G000270577

Cambridge Marketing Handbook: Digital

Cambridge Marketing Handbook: Digital

Steve Bax, Karl Meyer, and Neil Wilkins

Publisher's note

First published in Great Britain and the United States in 2013 by Kogan Page Limited in association with Cambridge Marketing Press.

120 Pentonville Road	1518 Walnut Street, Suite 1100	4737/23 Ansari Road
London N1 9JN	Philadelphia PA 19102	Daryaganj
United Kingdom	USA	New Delhi 110002
		India

www.koganpage.com

© 2013, Cambridge Marketing College.

The right of Cambridge Marketing College to be identified as the author of this work has been asserted by them in accordance with the Copyright, Designs and Patents Act 1988.

ISBN   978 0 7494 7063 0

British Library Cataloguing-in-Publication Data

A CIP record for this book is available from the British Library.

Design and layout by Cambridge Marketing College
Printed and bound by CPI/Antony Rowe, Chippenham, Wiltshire.

About the authors

This Handbook includes material created by some of the College's most experienced tutors, including Steve Bax, Karl Meyer and Neil Wilkins and has been edited by Charles Nixon and Les Shorthall.

Steve Bax

Steve is Managing Director of Bax Interaction, a Marketing Research and Strategy Consultancy with 25 years' experience at senior and board levels in small, medium and large organisations from a wide range of sectors in both B2B and B2C markets.

He is a qualified marketer with specialist skills in marketing research, strategic marketing planning, exhibitions and events management, direct marketing, managing change and building marketing teams. Previous roles include Chief Executive and Chairman for Foodex Meatex, the leading exhibition for the food industry, Marketing Manager for the Herbert Group of Companies and Marketing Research and Planning Manager for the Anglian Home Improvements Group. Steve is one of Cambridge Marketing College's most experienced tutors.

Karl Meyer

Karl has spent the past 20 years working within the Internet Industry in both Technical and Sales and Marketing Roles and was Director of Channel Marketing Strategy for WorldCom in EMEA. His roles took him across most of Europe and the Middle East, culminating in working for King Hussain of Jordan.

Karl is currently an Associate at SPICE.com – an on-line marketing agency focusing on delivering SEO, PPC, email marketing and social media marketing to deliver business growth to a wide variety of clients in the UK and overseas. His particular expertise is the use of Web Analysis and Social Media to target customers. He also runs an on-line toy business where he puts his knowledge of SEO and on-line marketing into practice.

Karl has an MBA from The Open University with a particular emphasis on International Enterprise Development and Knowledge Management and is a tutor for Cambridge Marketing College's Digital Programmes.

Neil Wilkins

Neil learnt his marketing with the likes of Orange, Natwest, BP Castrol and Ordnance Survey and now helps individuals and companies to communicate more effectively using strategic planning and dynamic tactical campaigns.

He is a Lead Tutor for Cambridge Marketing College's Digital Programmes and Course Director for the College's new Mobile Learning method of study. Neil is also the General Manager for the South West, driving the development of the College from the Bristol Study Centre.

Neil curates a Digital Marketing & Social Media topic on Scoopit – http://www.scoop.it/t/digital-marketing-social-networking

Charles Nixon

Charles began his career after studying History and Economics at Manchester University, a degree that he says gives him a long term approach to strategy. He was first employed as Government Relations Officer for Courtaulds (then the largest textile company in the UK) where he liaised with civil servants and politicians on government policy. Whilst at Courtaulds he was asked to explore the possibilities of the use of new mini computers in the field of market research and intelligence. This led to his founding Courtaulds' Office of Market Intelligence for its Consumer Products Group and establishing one of the first computerised marketing information systems in the UK.

After a short spell at the International Wool Secretariat as Senior Economic Analyst, Charles went to Warwick Business School (WBS) to take one of its first MBAs. Whilst there he helped write the Business Plan for the Warwick Science Park and so confirmed his interest in High Technology. Following WBS he joined Arthur Andersen Management Consultants (now Accenture) and spent time in Chicago and Geneva, before joining Mercury Communications the then embryonic rival to BT.

At Mercury, Charles was Head of Market Research and Market Planning helping the new company segment its market, plan for distribution, and research customer needs in order to introduce new products. In 1987 he moved to the City of London and joined Extel Financial in time for the Big Bang and the city revolution. These latter two posts gave Charles an insight in to the different ways UK companies approach the market and marketing.

Les Shortall

Les is an experienced strategist and business leader. Over a twenty-five year career in telecoms at UK, EMEA and global level, including B2B and B2C, he has held senior roles at Nortel, Philips, Simoco, Cambridge Broadband and Airwave (within Telefonica O2). As Head of Strategy Development at Airwave he worked with the Executive Team and Board to develop business strategy, drive the strategic plan implementation and set the partnering strategy.

In addition to tutoring at the College he is an associate consultant for Guardian News and Media. He holds an honours degree in engineering from Trinity College Dublin.

Contents

Word clouds produced through Wordle™ (www.wordle.net)

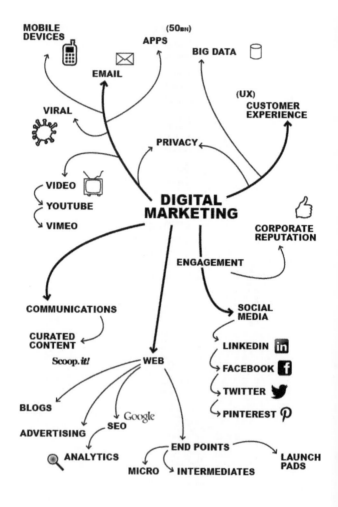

Infographic drawn by Lorna Brocklesby

Preface

Digital Marketing is more than just establishing a website. There is a complex array of channels and tools including email, online PR, social media, affiliate schemes, Apps and online advertising which together have the capability of helping a business achieve previously unseen growth.

No organisation can afford to ignore digital marketing.

Understanding what tools are available, how to use them and how to create and implement a co-ordinated digital campaign are essential elements in the marketer's toolbox. And it is a very fast moving area. This Handbook aims to introduce the key tools, set out how use them and how to create and implement a digital campaign. It has not been possible to cover every topic in full but advice is provided throughout on additional sources for more information on key topics. In addition, in this fast moving area of marketing, the reader must ensure they also keep in touch and up to date with new developments and innovations in the digital Graziano – it is all too easy to fall behind!

To keep up to date follow Scoop.it:
http://www.scoop.it/t/digital-marketing-social-networking

Introduction

The origins of the powerful set of online tools we now have at our disposal began in essence when Tim Berners-Lee and colleagues at CERN in Switzerland developed the concept of the world wide web (www). This allowed much more user-friendly access to the hardware backbone which was the internet, and established the protocol and basic building blocks (e.g. HTML) that allow us to create content in a way that can be read by anyone with a suitable reading programme (browser) anywhere on earth. It also allowed for development of the plug-ins, graphical and movie content, hypertext links, cookies and all the other characteristics we now take for granted.

In the 1990s the internet was regarded by some as a fad which would be replaced when the next big thing came along. Others regarded it as a subversive medium which would threaten our society. Now in a world with a population of 7.1 billion, in 2013, 41% of us have access to the internet. In the developed world, it is estimated that 78% of all households are connected to the internet. The number of smartphone users is on the rise too with an expected 2 billion owners by the end of 2013, with figures predicting that global smartphone penetration should pass 50% by 2017. It is fair to say then, that digital marketing has arrived!

Digital marketing provides an unprecedented opportunity for growth for businesses large and small. It allows organisations theoretically to achieve a global reach to new customers (and for competitors to do the same).

The term digital marketing is now in common use. Yet not so long ago in the 1990s, marketers would talk about 'new media' or internet marketing, online marketing or even 'e-marketing'. In this Handbook, we regard all these terms as equivalent to each other. Note however, that e-commerce (B2B and B2C transactions over the internet) and e-business (which includes all business processes that form part of the value chain) are distinct and beyond our scope here.

Digital marketing context

There has been a lot of hype over recent years about the advent of social media and how it has changed the world of marketing. However, before we dive into the detail of how to do digital marketing, let us put a little context to the numbers.

At the time of writing there are 1.11 billion users of Facebook, 225 million users of LinkedIn and over 200 million active accounts on Twitter, so there is no denying that social media has made a huge impact on the way the world communicates, both personally and professionally. With the exposure that social media can create, it is no wonder that companies such as Coca Cola have taken advantage of this fact with around 69 million 'likes'. Yet when compared with the total Facebook users or online population the most 'liked" company on the planet still only has less than 3% penetration.

World Population	World Population Online	Smartphone Owners	Number of accounts on Facebook	Coca Cola 'Likes' on Facebook
7.1 Billion	2.5 Billion	1.08 Billion	1.11 Billion	69 Million

It is also important to note, that despite all the hype that surrounds the increase in online sales and the effect it has had on our high street, it may be surprising to discover that internet sales currently only account for around 10% of total retail sales in the UK.

On the other hand as Figure 1 shows, the rapid increase year-on-year is evident, with the proportion of total sales having almost doubled in the past five years, making it an increasingly important factor to be taken into account. It also demonstrates how internet sales in countries across Europe have increased over the past five years.

Figure 1.1 Online retail market share 2008-2012 (Centre for Retail Research, 2013)

Marketers are recognising and responding to the opportunities these figures reveal as digital advertising spend increased by 14.4% to almost £4.8 billion in 2011 and then by a further 12.5% to near £5.42 billion in 2012 according to reports from the Internet Advertising Bureau UK (IAB, 2013).

The long-term growth of these digital advertising figures is shown in Figure 1.2. Whilst other media used for marketing have stayed constant over the past 10 years, digital marketing has consistently increased with companies allocating more and more of their budget to this area. It has now overtaken television but often advertising still exceeds online.

Sustained Long-term Growth

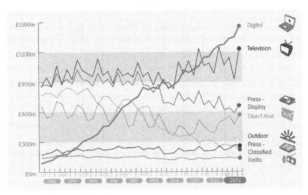

SOURCE: IAB / PwC Digital Adspend 2012 & WARC

Figure 1.2 Sustained long-term growth of digital marketing 2003-2012 (IAB, 2013)

These figures show that companies are acknowledging the power of digital marketing and its influence in the coming years will undoubtedly continue to grow, but its context should always be borne in mind. The offline physical world is still important and we are always dealing with human beings.

Chapter 1: Core Concepts
1.1 The digital marketing mix

When looking at the specific tools of digital marketing it is important to remember the marketing context and the fundamentals of the Marketing Mix. The marketing mix originally consisted of 4Ps: Product, Price, Place and Promotion. This was fine in the days when marketing was concerned with the marketing of physical products, as was the case for most of the period up until the late 1970s. However with the inexorable growth of the service sector the 4Ps were no longer sufficient. We needed to take account of the 'people' aspect of service plus the process by which customers enquired and bought the service. In addition given the very limited physicality of a service we needed to give greater emphasis to the packaging or physical elements. Consequently, People, Process and Physical Evidence were added to the marketing mix giving us the 7Ps, each of which has a digital aspect.

Subsequently the mix grew to 10Ps in order to be more explicit about the role of stakeholders:

- Public Opinion which explicitly takes into account the issue of Social Media
- Political Power and regulatory control (concerning us with the issue of internet privacy)
- Partners and stakeholders.

When considering each of the elements of the marketing mix, we need to bear in mind that they must not be considered in isolation. They need to be considered as a coordinated set of tools, any one of which will influence the others. Consequently, when introducing a new product, it is important to consider the pricing and the distribution of that product. If the market is not aware of it then the product will not be successful so promotion is essential. Coordination is therefore an important element in all marketers' tool kits. As we go through the marketing mix you always need to consider how each element can impact on the others.

Lets consider each of the 7Ps in a digital context starting with **Promotion.** Promotion comprises a range of tools that need to be selected and coordinated appropriately, all within the context of the wider Marketing Mix. The Promotions or Communications Mix includes not only the type of communication to be used but also selection of the right media. Are you going to advertise or use sales promotions; personal selling or direct marketing? If you are, are you going to use offline or online media or a mix? In addition Digital communications now adds the aspect of Dialogue. Whereas historically most marketing communications were one way, now with the advent of social media, there is a two-way dialogue to be managed by the company.

The **Product** P has arguably had the greatest overhaul as a result of the digital age. Whilst physical products are still manufactured and distributed much of the economy is now service based and can be digitised. In addition, many of what were seen as physical products have also been digitised causing carnage in the music industry and now reeking havoc in publishing. The creation of the App (mobile Application software) has created a world where almost any product benefit that can be digitised, will be. From 500 Apps in 2007 when the iTunes App store opened there are now over half a million Apps and there have been 50 billion downloads. There have been nearly as many from the Android Googleplay store.

People are still a key P in the marketing mix. Organisations must consider if they have the experience internally to plan and deliver digital and social networking activity. If not then some integration of third party specialists and agencies may be required for the initial research, auditing and planning as well as the ongoing delivery of campaigns and supporting tactical activity. Even in the digital world People are critical to good online customer service.

Then we have **Place**, where in an online space the organisation operates on a 24/7 365 days a year basis. The online experience never sleeps and as such organisations must prepare to deliver a consistent often irrespective of where in the world the visitor or customer is making contact.

This becomes particularly important when you consider that not all working weeks are Monday to Friday 9-5. In the Gulf States for example the traditional working week is Sunday to Thursday. It goes without saying that organisations in the Far East are operating on very different physical time zones to those in the Far West. The **Process** P is now critical in the way potential and returning customers can navigate around your website(s), be able to purchase or find information and share it with others.

This leads to a consideration of the back office systems and processes in a language and on terms appropriate to the customer. If, as is the case with most organisations, English is the predominant first online language, it is strategically important to consider how this might impact the customer experience if a priority target country or region does not have English, or the English alphabet, as a regularly used and acceptable language.

The choice of third party websites and social networking platforms is also an important consideration. The assumption of dominance of Facebook, Twitter and LinkedIn, may or may not be applicable to some target countries where locally popular social networks are significant. Examples of this can be seen in Italy and Brazil.

When planning to serve more than your local area or region it is very important to consider how customer service will be provided. Without a physical presence in a particular place there has to be a greater reliance on third party support and delivery services and an extension of the traditional supply chain as well as aftersales service. In this instance the careful selection of online messages and levels of promise must be in line with the digital promises and marketing to ensure the customer perceives the value of the promise in line with the actual experience received.

The broader the range of regions and countries served online, the wider the potential range of marketing, products and services required. The assumption that new regions will accept the existing way of marketing and doing business may not be valid.

Local product and service variants as well as website styles and tuning of digital marketing activity may be necessary.

Price is also a very important element of the digital mix. Prices in some categories (books and music) have dropped by up to 40% in recent years and in the online marketplace pricing is now used as a competitive differentiation tool. However, the challenge faced by all companies is not to over-utilise pricing and thereby drive down overall market value and threaten margins across the industry. Pricing must be in line and consistent with other elements of the mix and of course the brand value and positioning.

Pricing concepts have also had to be adapted to the internet as the concept of Free content has permeated much of what is 'for sale' on the internet. Software, services and support are often offered free at point of purchase but paid for either through advertising or through upgrades. Price comparison is also so much easier online.

Pricing can be a sensitive issue across international borders and the complexity of online legislation, regulations and local tax implications will all affect how organisations can do business.

There is also the opportunity to develop bespoke cost and pricing models throughout the supply chain with extranets opening up the chance to allow password access to restricted sites and bespoke price lists and product groups as appropriate. However pricing online is not always simple. There can be issues of transparency across borders, across markets and across customer segments. There is not always a requirement for the organisation to supply outside of its territory but this needs to be clearly communicated at point of purchase or before.

Physical evidence can be taken as referring to the customers' experience of accessing a website, including navigation, ease of use, value of content and overall 'stickiness'. Products bought online will mostly still require physical delivery for which the brand owner is still responsible, even if the initial transaction was made virtually. A joined up approach is required.

1.2 The magnificent seven

Key to the essence of effective digital marketing is planning. Without a plan to glue together potentially disparate activities and thinking, there is a real challenge to measure effectiveness and outcomes which in themselves are the required return on investment of time, resource and budget.

A good digital marketing plan should be integrated with broader marketing plans and further up-stream to corporate strategy and business objectives. An effective plan ensures the organisation invests in the right areas to grow the business through online and offline marketing.

The strategic issues facing marketers will include product definition, selection of range width and depth, brand building, management of the wider product portfolio and control and development of perception of quality within the overall product strategy.

With digital marketing there may be different numbers and types of participants in the value chain. The cost base, efficiency and power base in the chain may differ from the familiar chain a company is used to. All these things can make the mix more complex and need careful consideration when constructing and implementing an effective marketing strategy.

In addition to the 7Ps there are seven key priorities to consider when constructing your digital strategy and thinking about and planning digital marketing and social media for best effect:

- Relevance
- Advocacy
- Customer Journey
- Segmentation
- Integration
- Location
- Measurement

The careful blending of each of these seven elements turns the average online organisation into a world-class organisation providing engaging and measurable marketing to the most profitable customers.

Relevance is an essential ingredient in the mix. Companies can no longer publish what they want to say. Rather, they need to understand and publish what their customers want to hear. This is a small but crucial turnaround in emphasis that makes a fundamental difference to the way brands, products and services are perceived. Relevance is all about making it personal, customised, even to the point of bespoke, where the customer's perception is that everything they see, read and hear feels as though it was created just for them. At this point the engagement becomes not only a one-to-one between the organisation and its customers, but beyond to the customers' network of friends, family and colleagues.

This is termed **Advocacy** and, according to a number of research studies, is the most powerful form of online marketing, providing the highest returns of value to the organisation which harnesses it. Advocacy is the sharing of messages, conversations, branding and outcomes by customers with their networks and can result in up to ten times more effectiveness and eventual product purchase than a direct contact with the same organisation. Advocacy is now the staple diet of the strategic digital marketer seeking to ensure that everything they publish from blogs to tweets, e-newsletters to case studies, goes viral and spreads well beyond their first tier of contacts.

Such a focus enhances the concept of **Customer Journey**, the step by step touch points a customer has with an organisation. Advocacy can ensure they begin the customer journey at a deeper and more trusted level, potentially bypassing the initial stages of turning awareness into trust at the early steps in the buying decision making process.

Tying these threads together is the idea of **Segmentation**.

This is a realisation that different types of customer, based on age, demographics, location, lifestyle and need (and many other criteria) will interact very differently online and are seeking very different experiences. Companies who embrace segmentation can fine tune their offer and engagement with their segments to increase awareness and make the customer journey more relevant, which in turn can stimulate advocacy.

Where segmentation takes the digital marketing plan in the direction of multiple flavours, styles and tools, the concept of **Integration** brings everything back to a consistent, single strategic plan that allows prioritisation of effort, focus and budget. Using an integrated approach to planning, where content is duplicated and time and energy minimised by careful choreography of tactical and strategic activity, ensures that every step in the process can be measured, analysed and continually improved for the benefit of the customer and the organisation's return on investment.

And there is a relatively new kid on the block who appears set to change again the digital and social networking environment and provide as yet unseen benefits to those organisations who can work out effective ways of bringing it into the mix. This new concept is **Location**. Location has been present for many years in the form of GPS, Bluetooth and Mobile technologies but is only now becoming really relevant to organisations that have a geographic element to their products and services.

Ultimately all of these elements in the digital marketing process are only of value with effective **Measurement** and information that can be turned into decision-supporting intelligence. Decisions made from analytics and metrics that form part of every step in the process and customer journey are there to both enhance growth and reduce the risk of getting it wrong. Without measurement there is no effective plan and without an effective plan digital marketing and social networking become time consuming and low value activities. Harness these seven elements and the world is the organisation's oyster.

1.3 Offline versus online

It is important to understand that the majority of marketing still takes place offline. Online and digital media are rising fast but they still remain the minority of communications activity in terms of total spend. In addition for most consumers their exposure to offline marketing is still greater than to online marketing.

So we need to set online marketing in context and also set out some definitions:

Offline – all media that is not online such as as printed magazine or television advert. This can include some digital media such as digital billboards and DAB Digital Radio.

Online – all media communicated via the internet including the World Wide Web.

Digital – this is a wider definition that encompasses all digitally communicated media i.e. internet, web, mobile and offline digital such as broadcast and billboards.

With this in mind companies should remember that digital marketing must inherently link with existing offline sales and marketing activity, supporting real world campaigns, business development and sales visits.

Fragmentation of offline media

In the golden age of Advertising everybody watched the ITV (one channel), listened to the BBC and read a Newspaper. In addition there were magazines and poster sites. The result was that the majority of the nation could be reached by one or other of these main channels. However, with the coming of the digital production age it became easier to produce any of these media. The response was new companies set up to offer more targeted TV channels (Dave) or Radio stations (Classic FM) and specialist magazines. The result is that in the UK there are now over 800 radio stations, 500 TV Channels, 1,500 Newspapers and 1,900 magazines (Visit www.mediauk.com for up to the minute figures).

And most are available to advertise through. Added to this are the more direct media channels such as Direct Mail, door drops, or telesales. The result of this fragmentation and proliferation of media is that each single medium has limited reach and /or power to convince the audience by itself. Consumers have become more cynical about the content and more likely to miss the advert if it is not well targeted.

1.4 The digital consumer

Added to the proliferation of offline media and the myriad changes that are taking place in digital marketing and social media, today's consumer feels very busy. Home working, mobile devices, customer pressures and business demands all take their toll on our already hectic lives. And then in steps Social Networking to up the stakes and for many, dominate their very waking existence. Tweeting, checking friends' Facebook status, chipping in to LinkedIn message threads, trying again to create that elusive witty blog article, each of these potentially distracting activities adds up to a couple of hours a day for each and every one of us. Add in the established communications tool of choice for many, email, and the total number of hours increases to 3 hours a day.

The signs are that this is not going to go away and will actually increase. So what do you do? Simply accept fate and become submerged in the technology wave, or stop, think and plot a way through the barrage of digital noise?

The answer could be simpler than you think.

1.5 The concept of the digital hub

Your Digital Hub

Imagine a bicycle wheel. It has a hub at the centre and spokes linking it to the outer rim and tyres where contact is made with the surroundings. Effective digital marketing is very similar and helps to filter out irrelevant marketing tools and prioritise the most important, providing a clarity of experience and importantly a central point at which to encourage conversations, engagement and transactions.

You need to decide what is at the hub of your digital communications, online marketing and social networking. Where are you trying to direct customers, suppliers and partners? Is it to your website? Is it to specific social networks? Is it to your regular blog? With one element carefully positioned as the core of your communications everything else falls into place and knows its role... to feed people into the hub.

Strategically it is vital you decide this carefully depending on your overall objectives.

If it is to have more conversations with potential customers then perhaps your hub is one of your social networks, Facebook or LinkedIn, where you can engage with your targets on their terms and in their comfort zone. If your goal is to educate partners about your products and services you might need to drive them to particular pages on your website, in which case all of your digital marketing activity needs to point inward to there.

1.6 The digital marketing audit

Before diving into the Digital Hub you need to assess carefully your company's capabilities and resources. Too many companies plunge into digital marketing and especially Social Media with little understanding of what is required in order to do the job well. Many establish presences on social media platforms with little thought to the commitment needed to do a credible job. Many executives have seen this as a peripheral activity, establish a presence and then fail to maintain an up to date site or use the media to its fullest extent. This is equivalent to placing a magazine advert but failing to give the correct company address or phone number for enquiries.

Whilst there are 1.11 billion accounts on Facebook the company admits there are only 665 million active daily users (Associated Press, 2013).

Twitter is estimated to have 500 million accounts but only 200 million active users (Holt, 2013).

GooglePlus claims 500 million accounts though only 359 million active users and only 135 million actively posting to their accounts (Watkins, 2013).

So rather than spreading resources too thinly and consequently having a negative impact on corporate reputation it is important to carry out a Digital Marketing Audit.

There are five fundamental building blocks when you are assessing your current situation in digital marketing.

Weaving together the audit of these five elements gives you the platform from which to build a relevant, engaging, profitable and sustainable digital marketing strategy:

Organisation drivers
- Digital Strengths and Weaknesses of your organisation
- Assessment of previous campaigns
- Organisation objectives from which to build your digital targets
- Resources available, including budget, people and time
- Key Performance Indicators (KPIs) and what does success look like to your organisation?
- Unique Selling Propositions (USPs)
- What offline marketing needs to be integrated with digital?
- Who are the key stakeholders for your digital plan?
- How do you manage reputation and reduce risk?

Your people

- What staff resource do you have at your disposal?
- Is there appropriate knowledge and experience in the team or will you need to outsource?
- Do your online promises and marketing match your actual delivery?
- Establish internal cost constraints

Your technology

- What database and CRM systems are in place and are they appropriate?
- Do you have appropriate privacy and data protection protocols and processes?
- Which digital tools are already in use and what insights are coming from them?
- Do you have a digital dashboard collecting and reporting along the length of the customer journey?

World around you

- What competitor activity both online and offline will impact your planning and delivery?
- Do you know what partner and supplier activity works and what might be piggybacked?
- Competitor gap analysis can establish opportunities and potential threats
- Does your digital planning encompass the entire supply or value chain?
- What trends and future expectations of the competitor environment are appropriate to factor in?

The big picture

- What are the most appropriate digital tools within your planning timeframe?
- Have you considered the impact of Politics, Environment, Social, Technological, Economic and Regulatory factors (PESTER)?
- Prioritisation of customer or market segments to identify the reachable and most engaged customer groups
- Who are the key influencers in each market segment? This could be associations, media or customers
- Do different cultures, locations and languages across customer segments need different sub-plans?
- What are the key market and customer trends in behaviour, acceptance and expectations?

Addressing each of these in an initial digital marketing audit allows you to set up appropriate and relevant baselines from which to build strategic and tactical plans to achieve your online goals.

Chapter 2: Websites and SEO
2.1 Introduction

The company website is the most mature field of on-line marketing and historically one of the most important digital marketing tools. For the vast majority of online marketing the website is the chosen destination for customers and is the single most valuable piece of digital real estate you will ever own. This is the one thing over which you have complete control and can measure all of the activity on it.

As technologies have developed websites have evolved from the early basic 'brochure' style, static websites through transactional retail sites and are now much more interactive with each customer being able to witness a different, customised site.

Websites can operate in four different ways. They can be:

- End-points
- Launchpads
- Intermediaries
- Microsites

End Points are websites which users reach via searches and then complete their transaction at that site. Ecommerce websites are classic end point sites as their core aim is to capture the user and get them to buy. However some information sites may aim to ensure users stay within that site (news.bbc.co.uk could be seen to be an end-point). Hits onto an end point site are one way to measure the success of a marketing activity though conversion to a sale is also crucial and so the Conversion Ratio of inbound hits to sales is also a vital measure. Depending on the site, the Conversion Ratio can be as high as 20% or as low as 1% depending on the market sector and, crucially, the effectiveness of the marketing activity.

One major concern with all web based marketing is the phenomenon of **Bounce Rate**. Bounce occurs when a user clicks onto a website, scans the landing page, decides that the product/service/information is not relevant and immediately clicks away.

Bounce is a problem that is always going to occur but if the user has come to the web page via paid for (i.e Pay Per Click (PPC) advertising then a bounce is a 100% wasted payment. Therefore it is vital to measure, and understand Bounce Rate as part of any marketing activity.

Typically an end-point website will have a small number of pages/links that will be considered to be the goal. These might be checkout pages or contact/information request forms. Identifying how many customers reach these goal pages and the path they take through the site is crucial.

Launchpads are sites which aim to capture the user early but then direct them onwards to other sites. Search Engines are classic launchpads and earn money from the user leaving the site and going onwards to other content. However some commercial websites could be seen as launchpads. Motor manufacturer sites can be seen as launchpads as their aim it to persuade users to go to a dealership and/or request more information. Launchpads will have many goal pages and locations. Dwell time and customer path is probably of less relevance to these sites however accurate tracking of exits from the site is essential.

Intermediary sites, as the term suggests, are sites that offer elements of both end points and launchpads. They may contain significant content and will seek to attract users and returning users but will mainly earn their revenue from users leaving via paid for links. Blogs are a classic intermediary site but shopping comparison sites also act as intermediary sites and are one of the fastest developing areas of the internet (approaching saturation in some market sectors). These sites will probably pay for inbound traffic and aim to earn more money from outbound traffic (either via PPC ads or referral fees from sites such as Amazon). These sites expect a dwell time somewhere between those of an End Point site and a Launchpad site.

Customer paths through the website may be lengthy or very short. In general a short customer path tends to result in a relatively generic exit point (earning the site owner lower income) whereas a longer path (for example in a comparison site) will tend to provide a higher quality (and thus higher earning) exit point.

One interesting new development is the creation of multiple '**Microsites**'. These sites may (and in fact should) use the same delivery platform of hardware and software and will usually share some degree of corporate style but will offer users a different 'slice' through the organisation's information in a way that is much more targeted and focused.

Microsites could offer a slice through the corporate information either on a product by product basis or could be created to support a particular marketing campaign.

Microsites

The film industry was one of the first users of this method with each new film being provided with its own specific site (many of which are extremely comprehensive). The core reasons behind this innovation are twofold.

- To provide users an easy navigation to the relevant content (users want information on the latest Harry Potter rather than on Warner Brothers).

- To allow site owners to subdivide and separate users and traffic based on either specific marketing campaigns or products.

2.2 Websites with a purpose

In designing a web presence there are a host of considerations, many of which are common sense and arguably few actually require detailed technical implementation and skill sets. User friendliness is key. The aim is to provide a customer experience which envelopes and entices the user.

This is the 'customer journey', a key concept of the flow of experience the customer enjoys as they pass through brands, products and services on their way to an eventual outcome or purchase.

Whilst the 'old days' of website stereotypes are long since past for most organisations, care must be taken to avoid the 'corporate brochure'– placing text and images from the brochure online as well as overt selling when the user is seeking an interactive 'relationship' experience. Out of date information or 'page in development' must be avoided at all costs. Users are unlikely to return to unfinished websites. There is also the danger of using technology for technology sake. Simply because Flash and other bandwidth hungry technologies are available does not necessarily mean they are appropriate for every website.

Why are some websites dull, lifeless and out of date? Perhaps it is because they literally need a new lease of life. One of the key ways of enhancing a website is to let it grow and evolve by treating it as a member of your team:

Give it a job description – a reason for being part of the team

Invite it to team meetings – make it part of the team with a reporting slot and listen to it

Give it tasks and objectives – then you will know if it is performing

Do an annual review – see if it is really doing what it should

Keep it in the office conversation – listen to everything it tells you and respond accordingly

Too many businesses see their website as 'just another marketing tool' and a chore. Think of recruiting it into your team of people and it will take on a whole new lease of life. All the traditional improvement techniques like web analytics, search engine optimisation and social networking are important but to truly bring your website to life, treat it as you would expect to be treated yourself.

In some cases 'less is more' (e.g www.google.com) and care should be taken to balance style with content.

It is also imperative that navigation within the website is intuitive and effective with minimal numbers of 'mouse clicks' to move between zones. Once the web presence has been established the next consideration is to drive people towards it.

Transactions
For those organisations seeking to sell products and services through the web there are general rules to apply to ensure success. The 'shop front' is vitally important and must clearly enable product selection. The ordering process and fulfilment of the order must be a seamless flow of information both through the organisation and also through an updating response process to keep the customer advised of their order tracking.

Secure payment facilities are now widely available, accepting e-cash and credit and debit cards in a fully secure platform, many offering payment guarantees. Stories of web-crime continue in various forms in the media and whilst 'internet law' has yet to set precedence in some cases, in general, current law practice still applies. Contracts made at the point of purchase are still legally binding. This does however become more complex when dealing across country or continent boundaries where different legal practice may apply. Legal disclaimers are essential to protect both the buyer and seller and these must be highly visible at a point early in the transaction process.

It is vital that companies protect their trademarks and register all URLs (web addresses) that are relevant to their master brand. As in traditional media, copyright exists on all original works and therefore the source of any third party material must be attributed by the company using it.

2.3 Search Engine Optimisation (SEO)
Arguably the most important method of driving traffic to a website is an effective search engine position.

This can take many forms from simply good website design using a large number of appropriate key words in the content, to paid position for a fee (pay-per-click or pay per impression) advertising.

Earlier forms of search engines deeply analysed keywords buried inside the coding for the pages, and meta tags or descriptions and titles. Now search engines have developed into sophisticated automated applications that 'read' the content of the website and position each site according to the appropriateness of its content relative to others. Such applications include 'robots' and 'spiders' which regularly revisit sites for reassessment.

Search Engine Optimisation is the process of getting the best ranking for a website. Ideally on the first page of the search results. As is observable to the most casual of internet surfers there are millions of hits now for any search and most users only look at the first page. Websites and other online communication media are displayed by search engines through a complex algorithmic process of which SEO is a composite, contributing in two major ways:

- By trying to improve the volume of traffic to the website by optimising the relevance of the results of the search; and
- By more accurate targeting to the specific enquires.

The ultimate objective of optimisation is to be at the top of any search engine listing from an enquiry. SEO refers to organic searches as opposed to sponsored links. The former is the 'natural' relevancy of a website for a particular product or information source in relation to others. The latter is paid for advertising.

All search engines frequently alter their algorithms for a top ranking. At Google this is approximately once every 2–4 weeks and is conducted by sending out bots (robots), or crawlers also called spiders, which interact with websites' root directories.

Like anything in business, a strategic approach is required such as: what objective the website wants to attain (hits, sales, referrals), taking on board the type of product service or information the website has to offer; and what kind of search engines to concentrate on.

Google for example is currently the most favoured search engine in Europe, which has earned them the term "to Google" as a generic verb for web searches. However there are others (Yahoo, Bing, etc.) and specialist industry search engines (see Section 2.4).

Search Engines are increasingly important due to a combination of socio-cultural and technological lifestyle reasons: people are more time precious, in part due to an increasing array of leisure choices available; our access and reliance on internet interconnectivity is becoming more and more pervasive; and two key trends have taken distinct shape over the past few years: mobile technology and the growth of social networks.

Organic ('natural') search
Each search engine has its own set of algorithms which it does not disclose, although most will give pointers to what approaches site owners can take to optimise their rankings. Some such as Google allow users to predict their placing using queries on the search engine.

It has generally been held that searches appear higher in ratings when Metatags (information inserted into the 'head' area of your web pages) containing keywords are present. In fact, as we have already noted many engines, including Google, do not use metatags in ranking sites. The metadata is useful however, as this will be seen by the searcher when the listings are returned, hence a sensible choice of terms, especially page titles is important.

Other techniques should be considered: content specific protocols, such as removing index barriers (e.g. a Flash landing page with a large sized file picture). For example, a film review website with large, high quality images would find it difficult to be ranked highly if it took particularly long for pictures on the landing page of the website to download.

Inbound links have been the most important single factor rated by Google, but in more recent times, the importance of links has been downgraded heavily in favour of original, fresh content.

Marketers also need to be aware of terms such as 'Black Hat SEO' and 'White Hat SEO'. The former refers to unscrupulous or deceptive ways that organisations and individuals improve rankings, and these are disapproved of by the search engines. A simple example would be including lots of keywords in a manner invisible to the site user e.g. white text on a white background, intended only to attract search engines.

Black Hat SEO

In 2011, JC Penney received a 90-day penalty from Google when it was discovered they were using link farms (which are websites created solely to increase the popularity of another website by increasing the number of links to it) to artificially boost their Search Engine rankings – rankings for keywords dropped several pages. The retailer caught the New York Times' attention because they had the number one position on search engines for a multitude of keyword searches from trophy keywords such as 'home decor' and 'furniture' to longer, obscure tail keywords such as 'grommet top curtains'.

White Hatters are defined as being ethical and responsible SEO players who produce long lasting results.

Paid inclusion

It is common for search engine companies, e.g. Yahoo, to be paid a fee (usually a one off or yearly subscription) by a company or individual in order to be included in their index. The rationale is to maintain credibility amongst website users in order for them not to be exposed to multifarious adverts. Blogging sites with high volumes of traffic have championed this technique.

While Google initially declared it would not offer paid inclusion, it now does so with some search functions such as Hotel Finder.

PPC (Pay Per Click)
One of the quickest though most expensive means to capture traffic to websites is PPC advertising. PPC, as the name suggests, are adverts placed on other websites (or potentially emails) that direct users to your site. Google's Adwords is the most well known PPC service though all search engines provide a similar service.

The essentials of PPC are:

- The company selects the key words or phrases that they believe users will use within their searches.
- They create an advert (text or graphic) that is designed to attract the user.
- The company decides how much each click on the advert is worth and sets a maximum CPC (cost per click).
- The advert distributor (e.g. Google) places these adverts on pages either in their search engine (Search Ads) or on the websites of content providers who subscribe (Content Ads).
- Usually multiple adverts will be placed with the position and ranking defined by the amount the company is willing to pay (Pay more and get a better position on the page).
- If a user clicks on the advert they are directed to the company's site and the company pays the distributor (e.g. Google). If the ad is on a content page then the distributor will split the revenue with the content provider.
- An advertiser may bid and 'buy up' certain key words or phrases relevant to their product or service, with the price they have to pay depending on the demand for the word. This is known as Cost per Click (CPC).

Google AdSense offers an alternative advertising model, which matches ads to your site's content and you earn money whenever your visitors click on them. It has two forms:

- **AdSense** for content automatically crawls the content of web pages and delivers ads that are relevant to the audience. The idea is that the ads are so well matched that readers will find them useful and not intrusive. A mobile variant also exists.

- **AdSense for search** allows website publishers to provide Google web and site search to their visitors and to earn money by displaying Google ads on the search results pages.

Accountability

The growth in digital marketing spend has been continuous due to the shift of marketing budgets being directed from offline to online activities. One of the key influencers of this is the ease with which spend can be made accountable and evaluated. For example, with Google AdWords it is possible to spend as little as £10 on a campaign or £100,000. The flexibility of this method also means that it is relatively easy to tweak a campaign during its operation by monitoring items such as Click Through Rates (CTRs). PPC campaigns can and do sit alongside organic SEO strategies.

Search and display

If search and display are tracked together, then the advertiser and agency can really understand their consumer's path to conversion. For example, a user engages with an advert for the first time. Then three days later they use a search engine to look for the product name they remembered seeing on the advert. They click on the PPC sponsorship link but do not go through to purchase. Finally, on day eight they convert via a different ad on a different publisher, making a purchase on the advertiser's website.

Traditionally, the conversion would only be awarded to the last ad or keyword seen. But when the whole path is analysed, we see the value of each touch point along the path. The trends of each of the channels and publishers that drive the conversions can be shown, and their individual media attribution values calculated – eventually enabling marketers to plan their budgets better across search and display in order to achieve the best return on investment.

However, with the multitude of search engines and bid management tools in use, a technology solution is still required to enable wide-scale search and display integration.

2.4 Vertical search engines and web portals

Vertical search engines (VSEs) are created to meet the need to search within a subject sector. These focus on the particular information needs of a specific market segment.

Due to the rapid speed at which the internet is transforming, VSEs are set to grow and could drive the next iteration of the internet cloud. Clouds are where computer and data is stored and managed by experts. For example, there are search engines that crawl consumer health sites – they serve a particular need (health information) for a specific market segment (the consumer, and sometimes the health practitioner).

The advantages of VSEs to the marketer relate to the simple old adage that in business 'time is money'. VSEs save time in relation to relevancy so the marketer has more options and tighter accuracy in targeting. If we take the example of health further, the establishment of a Healthline accessible on the vertical search would increase ratings amongst B2B and B2C users.

All the best health sites in the world would want to be associated and be found by the VSEs. B2B professionals and customers alike might want to personalise the site to their usage which on the whole enhances the interface by making navigation easier for other health topics.

Marketers should be clear to distinguish the difference between a vertical search engine and a portal.

Vertical search engines are about assisting informed and confident decisions. By presenting connections across products, messages and services, in front of the right audiences, they can be defined as sub components of search engines that focus on specialised and specific content.

The content within the search engine is sorted out in accordance to specific criteria such as location, type of service or object, research surveys, etc.

It is widely anticipated that increased usage of vertical search engines will be spearheaded by the B2B market as professional bodies and institutes work towards strategic partnerships and build mutual relationships to foster efficient and cost effective work practices.

A web portal has a different look and feel from a VSE although some of their functional features may overlap.

Web Portals were the natural progression for early internet based companies in the early 1990s such as Netscape, Walt Disney, Alta Vista, Hotbot, and Excite who wanted to have a piece of the internet market. The overall strategy was to increase options and features so that users spent more time on the internet real estate which increased activity, traffic and eventually revenue.

Web portals present information from diverse sources in a unified and consistent way with access control and procedures for multiple applications, such as mobile and email facilities.

In order to find a Vertical Search Engine, a good starting point would be to use a query at a general (horizontal) search engine e.g. health vertical search or health portal. Nevertheless, the market is changing rapidly with Google's introduction of Google CSE (customised search engine) which allows the customer to search for a topic or item, receiving results more concentrated and relevant to the search query. Another company making waves in this sector is Eurekster, who have also adopted a user friendly approach to vertical searching.

Below are some samples of specific search genres:

- Answers Searching
- Computer Search Engines
- Domain Searching

- Financial Search Engines
- Government Search
- Invisible Web
- Legal Search Engines
- Mailing Lists
- Medical Search Engines
- Newsgroup Search
- Science Search Engines
- Shopping Search
- Travel Search Engines
- WAP Search Engines
- Other Specialty Services

2.5 Customer optimisation and long tail content

There are different stages in customer engagement that will make SEO more or less relevant at different points. This idea is called Customer Optimisation and is actually as important as SEO in terms of the actual experience the customer enjoys after the SEO has worked and brought them to the website. Different things will apply to their experience depending on where they are in their customer journey:

Awareness stage – reaching customers who would otherwise not be aware of the organisation, its brands, products and services

Acquisition stage – turning this awareness into the buying process and converting them from aware to customers

Retention stage – ensuring existing customers are not just old customers but actively up-buying and cross-buying and behaving as loyal advocates. Optimisation must ensure it addresses all three stages for the benefit of the search engine and also the customer experience. A key method of achieving this is called **Long Tail Content**.

Long Tail Search Phrases are one of the key search ranking criteria that Google and the other dominant search engines are now using to rate your site against the competition.

Long Tail is vital to search engine optimisation because it equates a specific reference to a page for the spiders.

Specificity is the key ingredient. The longer the search phrase the fewer people will search using it but those who do will be perfectly targeted towards the appropriate page on your website. The search engines are equating the value of 100 people coming to your web page and it being relevant to the financial value of that visit to you. They would rank lower a search optimised page that is less specific and generates 100,000 people but for whom the actual experience on the page is irrelevant. In long tail content and long tail search, less is more as it equates to a higher value per visitor.

2.6 Will the next generation of web be driven by search?

There is currently a debate about whether Cloud Marketing will be driven by search. The current search model in digital marketing assumes the user has most control. They know what they are looking for as they input their key word or long tail phrase into their trusted search engine. Out pops the search engine result, a list of organic results based on the quality of web page the engine assumes will be of value to you and a host of sponsored links where those vying for your valuable attention bid for space to be seen before their competitors.

It is a simple and proven model that works a treat for all concerned and generates billions of dollars each year for content providers, engines, brokers, advertisers and wholesalers.

So will this be the logical model that Cloud Marketing will evolve from?

That would be an evolution but in some ways a shame because it misses an opportunity for Cloud Marketing to create its own revolution, putting the driving force not in the hands of a searching user but in the relevant situation in which they find themselves bringing into play location, purchase history, activity and 'likes', etc. This could open up all sorts of experiential opportunities for creative marketers, driving new digital, virtual and real world experiences for the user based on their location, their preferences and their past behaviours.

Search would be a simple option to fuel the cloud, but creative marketing minds may be able to develop so much more.

2.7 Internal communications

It is also worth bearing in mind that internal websites or intranets can revolutionise internal communications. The base principles of internet websites follow those for intranets. They can help employees feel informed and part of the organisation, improve productivity and reduce inefficiency. If they are kept regularly updated the intranet can ensure all employees have the latest information in a consistent manner whilst reducing paper and the print costs normally associated with printed employee newsletters.

The more advanced intranets allow for collaborative project working and can act as a company archive resource. However, websites are just one element of digital marketing and they should be supplemented as part of a wider mix with elements like e-newsletters.

2.8 The future and behavioural targeting

Online behavioural advertising is a way of using information about people's web browsing activity to serve them advertisements based upon these interests. Users are assigned a unique, randomly-generated number to their browser to preserve anonymity. Then their categories of browsing activity are matched with advertising. But from September 2009, advertisers have had to allow customers to decide whether they want their browsing activity to be made known; an opt-out must be provided. See Chapter 8 and www.youronlinechoices.co.uk

New initiatives are constantly being put into place such as Search Retargeting that serves ads across the Yahoo Publisher Network based on a Yahoo user's prior Yahoo searches. It works by Advertisers being able to retarget a customer who has conducted a search with a more tailored proposition. For example, if a user searches for the keyword 'sandals', signifying strong purchase intent, an advertiser can target that user with a tailored display ad for footwear.

Sky also used this technique to tailor their advertising to viewers' interests, creating a uniquely powerful way of communicating with them. By implementing behavioural targeting technology on the Sky site, this served tailored advertising to Sky viewers who were later exposed to these adverts on other media sites like Yahoo! and MSN.

Chapter 3: Digital Communications
3.1 Email

Beyond the 'awareness creation' stage of the typical advertising models we need to integrate our tactics with direct marketing to known customers. A key tool in this is email marketing.

The number of worldwide email accounts is expected to increase from an installed base of 3.9 billion in 2013 to nearly 4.9 billion by year-end 2017 (The Radicati Group Inc, 2013). A typical corporate email user sends and receives over 100 email messages per day – though the growth rate in the number of emails sent and received per day is slowing down due to the rapid rise in other forms of communications, particularly instant messaging (IM) and social networks.

Consider these two examples to see how broad email marketing can be:

- A large consumer goods company sends special offers to millions of potential customers, tracks the responses and sends context-sensitive follow up messages with sophisticated tracking and data collection.

- A small professional consultancy sends personal emails to senior executives as a prelude to calling them and seeking a meeting.

In fact, it is difficult to think of an organisation which might not use emails in some form or another as a way of engaging with stakeholders. According to a survey carried out by B2B Marketing in 2011,the following statistics applied to UK B2B Marketers:

- Email remains the most popular marketing tool, used by 90% of respondents.

- The most common primary marketing objectives of email are to 'create leads for sales conversion' (42%), 'drive direct sales' (19%) and 'build brand' (16%).

- Email marketing is set to benefit most from an increase in investment for lead-orientated activity, with 55% of marketers saying they will spend more on this channel.

Advantages and disadvantages

Whereas websites tend to be a 'pull' technology, where users pull the information off the site when they need it, email tends to be a 'push' technology where content is actively sent to users.

This has both significant advantages and disadvantages for email:

- the ability of marketers to control what information is delivered and when it is delivered is enhanced;
- the delivery of content is at a very low cost;
- modern email clients can offer rich graphical content – virtually to the same level of control as a web page; and
- tracking codes can be inserted to identify when an email is opened and what links are used; but
- the low cost can tempt senders to send more and more frequent emails and users can (and often do) object to being 'bombarded' with emails and overuse of email can result in senders being blacklisted as spammers.

The majority of email marketing has until recently been used to promote websites (on-line to on-line marketing). However there have been significant advances using the email facility on smartphones to send discount codes or vouchers to users' mobiles which can then be used in retail outlets (see Chapter 5).

There are a number of key measures used to analyse email effectiveness:

- **Open rate** – the percentage of subscribers who open an email
- **Click rate** – what percentage click on a link within the email
- **Unsubscribe rate** – how many users unsubscribe from a mailing list

- **Bounce rate –** bounce has a different metric compared to web analytics. Within email marketing this refers to emails that are 'bounced' back undelivered by the recipients' mail servers. This is similar to the rate of undelivered and returned mail with a physical mail drop. However once a link within an email has been clicked any further 'bounces' refer to the act of the user returning immediately from the website.

It should be noted that most email marketing relies on tagging links and images with additional codes (or script) that is activated when the email is opened (and so requests images or code), and when links are clicked. Many email clients will automatically refuse to download images with tracking codes and so the Open Rate and Click Rate for email marketing are often large underestimates.

Email clients

An email 'client' is a piece of software used to manage email campaigns. Anyone contemplating any sort of volume email campaign will need to automate, monitor and measure the campaign in some way, and email clients provide for these features and much more. A good software email client will offer the following features:

- An easy-to-use visual interface for importing text, pictures and graphics into HTML templates – important to give messages visual impact.
- Does not require HTML programming experience or web development skills.
- Selectable timing of mail delivery, helping to create maximum impact.
- Existing customer databases can be uploaded into the system; users can be selected by searching for keywords and targeted with relevant promotional communications.
- Advertisements and/or promotional links can be placed within the mail, directing traffic through to relevant pages on a customer's (or third party's) site.

- Each hyperlink within an email can be assigned a keyword to describe the type of link included, enabling a customer to track an individual user's visit record(s).
- Test for compatibility with different e-mail reading programs (e.g. mobile devices).
- Support for opt-out requests.

Not all e-mail readers (e.g. Microsoft Outlook) will render an e-mail the same way, and Mac users may see things differently from Windows users, so testing and previewing is vital in ensuring a high level of both recipient acceptance but also engagement.

Email marketing can be seen as a facet of customer relationship management (CRM). The advantages of email for marketing may include:

- Much lower cost than postal equivalents
- As a direct response tool, it encourages immediate action
- Campaigns can be put together more quickly
- Segmentation (especially by response) and personalisation are easier
- Tracking and testing are far easier online

In common with postal direct mail, the marketer can expect some resistance to contacting people by e-mail. Not everyone likes to receive mail from organisations, especially if they do not regard themselves as having a relationship with that organisation. One person's carefully crafted, well targeted e-mail campaign is another's 'junk mail' or 'spam'. Many people at home and at work feel they already get too much e-mail, so there are hurdles to be overcome in getting e-mails opened, getting them read and getting them acted upon.

Some obvious advice for maximising your chances are:

- Have an enticing subject line
- Consider appropriate length and frequency

- Make it easy to read/include a table of contents, with brief descriptions of what is included and links to more information (usually on your website)
- Make it personal and casual

Etiquette and the law

There are a number of legal requirements surrounding the use of mailing lists – primarily these are incorporated within the Data Protection Act (DPA) and require names and email addresses to be used only with the permission of the recipient and only for the purposes agreed by the recipient. The general requirements of the DPA are common to all forms of commercial use of customer data and apply equally on the internet as within the 'real world'. See the Law Handbook for more on the DPA.

There are also matters of etiquette in the use of email and these can readily be summarised by the general principle "do unto your customers as you would expect to be done by your suppliers" i.e. do not annoy with excessive emails, do not share or sell data, do not send irrelevant emails but equally do not become overfamiliar.

For more on email:

A full list of all the terminology used within email marketing can be found at http://emailmarketingpro.org/email-marketing-terms/

3.2 Online PR

PR is the broadest and perhaps least understood of the tools in the digital marketing toolkit. Often taken to mean 'press relations' as in press releases, equally often it is given such a wide definition that it includes trade shows, sponsorship, investor relations and so on.

We shall not debate this here, except to say that digital marketing impacts on PR just as much as other areas of marketing.

Let's take a common definition of PR from the UK Chartered Institute of PR:

"The management of reputation, the planned and sustained effort to establish and maintain goodwill and mutual understanding between an organisation and its publics".

The word 'publics' covers a very wide range of people and organisations who are interested in or affected by an organisation. These include: employees, customers, investors, regulators, suppliers and so on. Digital techniques have really come into their own to achieve management of communication with such diverse groups. Online PR can be said to leverage the network effect of the internet, where leverage is defined as the value, financial or otherwise, to the organisation.

Since PR is often about people talking about people, the internet gives them many more opportunities to do so. Generally, PR practitioners wish to maximise the number of times their organisation is mentioned in a favourable context. New digital tools such as blogs, RSS feeds, social networks, etc. offer just such opportunities.

However, just as with offline PR, the control the organisation has over what is being said about them is minimal. Online the picture is much more challenging. Individuals can come and go, making untrue, offensive or otherwise damaging posts and then disappearing, leaving their posted information on the web where it may stay for years. e.g. when Mars started a forum for their Skittles product, it did not expect that someone would post an assertion that Skittles causes cancer.

It is vital to factor in resource and strategic pre-formed responses to such scenarios. The benefits within the social networking mix of digital-PR are significant when positive advocacy from loyal customers makes the most noise but there will be inherent negativity that also needs to be managed proactively as part of the process.

A key issue here is that people now have many more choices of where they get their information from. They can, often in a few seconds, access multiple opinions on any topic from all around the world. They no longer have to believe what the organisation has told them e.g. through a press release. They may identify influential individuals whose opinions they listen to, for example by 'following' them on Twitter or Technorati. They may belong to special interest groups such as those on LinkedIn, or take part in discussion forums such as the investors groups on Yahoo! Finance. Getting your message to stand out among this noise can be challenging to say the least.

Pro-active techniques to promote your message

On the other hand we now have powerful tools to help us promulgate our message and reach out to many more people. SMS and MMS communications can be issued via contact directories. E-mails can be sent to large distribution lists instantly, and provide more information or follow up through hypertext links. We can build links back to our websites.

Newsletters and e-zines (electronic magazines) can be distributed to subscribers and notifications issued to those who have requested an alert on a particular topic or event. Our comments can be posted manually or automatically on blogging sites. Our news releases will show up on Google Alerts, and all of this activity does our search engine placement no harm.

Traditional PR (narrowly defined as seeking editorial coverage of your products and services), can still be enhanced and made far more efficient through digital marketing tools. Journalist contacts can be managed efficiently through databases and e-mailed with only relevant stories in far less time than previously. They can be reached through specialist tools set up to distribute news, such as PRWeb, BusinessWire and PR Newswire.

An important part of success in PR is having a good database of contacts in the various media, so that communications and news can be tailored to the needs of particular publications or broadcasters.

It is also important for monitoring upcoming features to which a contribution can be planned. In the digital world, such databases inevitably are available online, usually by subscription. In this way, they can be kept more up to date than printed directories and can provide search facilities and direct links to publications or e-mail addresses. They also often provide contact management tools. One of the best known tools of this type is Factive Media Relations Manager which claims to link its traditional and social media with journalist and blogger data (www.dowjones.com/collateral/files/factiva-for-communicators-factsheet.pdf).

For other examples of tools that can be used in online PR, see the relevant sections in this Handbook on RSS, SEO, Blogs, Podcasts, and Social Media.

Media centre

Journalists, bloggers and other publishers will expect to be able to get hold of certain information about companies and their brands. The easier it is to find, the more likely the company is to be featured in news stories, reports and articles. The most popular way to provide this information is through a virtual press office or 'media centre' on the website which can make virtual press kits available on demand.

Examples of content in a media centre would include:

- Standard descriptions of the company
- Company ownership and subsidiaries
- Company officers and their biographies
- Product range
- Images of people, products and applications
- Archive of press releases

Techniques to monitor coverage and react to events

In the digital world, communications are much more frequent, more informal and accessible to almost everyone. For these reasons, it is perhaps inevitable that comment (or gossip) will be less guarded and less respectful.

Posting critical comments about organisations is even seen by consumers as a valid tactic to get their way, or to exact revenge for some perceived shortcoming. What is being said, how often and by whom are essential items to monitor. For many low profile companies, getting mentioned/noticed at all is the biggest problem, and coverage in the various media will generally be positive. On the other hand, large companies such as Microsoft or Tesco, will attract mixed coverage.

Coverage gained can be monitored through online media monitoring (the equivalent of the press clippings of old). Companies such as Vocus and Cision have sophisticated offerings in this market. Google Alerts can be set up, but for more detailed analysis see www.gigaalert.com.

Virtual forums

Since the best PR is a two way dialogue (see Grunig & Hunt's model of two way symmetric communication), companies wishing to interact with their stakeholders more directly may set up company forums to facilitate dialogue between interested parties and to some extent the company itself (Grunig & Hunt, 1984). These are sometimes referred to as message boards, chatrooms or newsgroups, but generally have a 'threaded' structure so that users can 'converse' on particular topics, find topics by searching the thread index and so on.

Organisations wishing to engage with such social communities have to decide whether they are going to take part as individuals, or as representatives of their organisations. A key principle of social media is transparency. For example, users do not like to see commercial messaging thinly disguised as comment. There have been many examples of companies who have fallen foul of this informal rule. On the other hand, customers do appreciate genuine personal contact with senior executives of large corporations. Robert Scoble at Microsoft and Scott Month at Ford are well-known pioneers of using social media to the advantage of their companies by taking a more open approach to communications and effectively inventing a new form of PR.

The value of social network marketing as a PR tool

Social Network Marketing, or Engagement Marketing, has revolutionised the way organisations communicate with the consumer and extends the tools available to carry out relationship marketing. But it is not always organisations that try to use this to gain stronger relationships and public support. Social networking is used very well by journalists, professionals and celebrities too.

For example, David Beckham has teamed up with Samsung to promote the Galaxy Note mobile phone by showing off his aiming skills. By kicking balls at a wall of drums Beckham recreates the melody of Beethoven's 'Ode to Joy.' He then uploaded the video straight to his 18-million-fan strong Facebook page, highlighting the phone's crystal-clear display and superfast connectivity.

Stephen Fry is a very popular 'Tweeter', along with most celebrities, who are not doing anything different from organisations. They use social networking to communicate and engage with their own 'consumer' to promote themselves. This supports the notion that personalisation and conversation is the essence of networking rather than direct advertising. However, in the world of celebrity there is a distinct advantage in that people want to listen.

Most organisations do not have that luxury so marketers and communicators, who strive to understand the needs, desires and wants of their customers, are looking at how to use social network marketing to conduct dialogue between brand and consumer. This dialogue is essential to give marketers the opportunity to gauge opinion, satisfaction levels and desires to enable us to provide a better proposition. Social networking helps organisations achieve this as it allows marketers to seek dialogue with its customers and if an organisation is prepared to listen to the feedback, it can change its behaviours accordingly to meet their needs. Rather than feeling dictated to, the consumer is putting more pressure on us to listen.

Through social media tools we are learning how to listen.

This is something that Richard Dixon, Director of Customer Optimisation, Black Sun commented on in an article for Marketing magazine: "Analysis by McGraw Hill has proven that brands that invest in their customer relationships will grow 275% quicker than those who do not. Indeed, one can already see in some corporate results those brands focusing solely on price promises and value are suffering, while those that engage customers and focus on value are outperforming their peers." (Dixon, 2011).

Organisations that are engaging with social network marketing tools have been labelled as 'networked enterprises'. These organisations are expertly implementing this exercise into wider customer relationship strategies and are experiencing growth and reward for their time and investment as a result. This focus on the consumer involves in-depth research and constant re-evaluation of every aspect of a social networking campaign. In fact, research and evaluation form the very essence of the social media marketing process. We look at this in more detail in Chapter 4.

3.3 Blogs

Blogging has become a tool of choice for many organisations seeking to share their true values and innovation with the world.

Originally blogging took the form of a personal oriented narrative with a reflective nature, akin to a diary, commenting or shedding insight on a situation, scenario or opinion. The ease of use, flexibility and accessibility of communications fostered by the internet made the blog easy to share. As bloggers also function as key hubs within the communications model, doubling as opinion leaders in some cases and opinion formers in others, they have often been at the centre of the world of the early adopter. A classic example of the latter is the renowned Robert Scoble. Blogs amalgamate the uniqueness and power of personal publishing, which can be intoxicating and engaging, as well as harnessing the ability to influence and inform communities.

Although Justin Hall, a student in USA in 1994 is considered the founder of personal blogging when he started to blog commentaries about his web discoveries, it is Jorn Barger who coined the term weblog in 1997, on his site www.robotwisdom.com which consisted of a collection of his eclectic articles and websites. Two years later, Peter Merholz shortened the term to web-blog or blog for short. Evolving from this word 'blog', is the term blogosphere which in essence is the environment from which bloggers communicate and share. Implicitly referring to the internet, this term also implies the collective community of all blogs.

The potency of blogging is that it can be seen as representing some kind of consensus amongst the public or in the context of trade consumers. Within this component of personal blogging is the term 'Microblogging', which entails a detailed moment by moment commentary, expressing instantaneous feelings and thoughts. Micro-blogging is championed by social networks such as Twitter, which itself is increasingly being integrated into third party platforms e.g websites, mash-ups and mobile phones.

Web marketing 2.0 and blog advertising
The distinction between a blog and a website has become increasingly blurred. This in fact is a phenomenon of web 2.0 which is the culmination and integration of several other platforms into one with blogging sites supporting widgets, video-blogs or Vlogs etc. Web 2.0 is all about maximising and accentuating the potential of social networks, erasing the distinction between work and play, between business and leisure. It is for this reason that more and more companies and brands want to engage in dialogue with their customers. McKinsey's 2011 study of business use of social media reported that, among companies using Web 2.0 for customers-related purposes, the key benefits include the following (Chui, et al. 2012):

- 63% report more effective marketing
- 50% report increased customer satisfaction
- 45% report reduced marketing costs
- 25% cite increased revenue

A key word associated with blogs is 'traffic' and as a result some blogs feature advertising which may fund other ancillary activities, depending on the author or, they may reflect the concerns or important causes of the author. Popular writers are able to offer a lot of traffic, which attracts advertisers. The secret for the marketer then becomes how to aggregate this traffic. The following are some sites that provide insight into how the advertising industry is engaging with this medium by acting as intermediaries or affiliates:

Blogads (www.blogads.com) – allows you to match advertisers with bloggers. Once registered advertisers choose you, you either accept them or not, depending on your personal bias. Running blogads is free but the service keeps a percentage of your earnings.

Commission Junction (www.cj.com) – is an affiliate network and one of the most renowned players in the market. They give advertisers the ability to partner with thousands of advertisers – users can choose to partner with as many advertisers as they wish.

Google Adsense (www.google.com/adsense) – provides unobtrusive advertising on your website based on the contents of your blogging page.

As the old dichotomy between push and pull marketing recedes, the key ingredient in the equation now is to grab attention. This in part has been the drive of the new business models for other social networks such as Myspace, Facebook, YouTube and others whereby the number of users gives commercial value to the organisation. At present there are attempts to standardise how web blogs are ranked. The American company Technorati has established itself as a reputable source in assembling credible data of rankings in the blogosphere world.

Although blogs are of use to all industries, they have had significant repercussions for the media sector, most notably with radio and newspapers.

Nowadays, most journalists have online blogs they use to expand on topical news items, which in turn encourages readers to interact with the journalists, comment on their stories and link to their blogs.

Corporate blogging

Businesses have been quick to realise the potential of blogging and 'corporate blogging' has steadily increased. Such blogs have been used for both internal and external communications making use of the internet and intranets.

Corporate blogging

Dell Corporation is a company that has harnessed this medium. When (in 2006) an influential customer was not content with Dell's customer service standards he voiced his grievance by starting a blog. Dell was later forced to recall a number of their laptop computers and the blog was the first port of call for most customers as opposed to the phone (whose lines were blocked). Later as the furore subsided Dell launched ideaStorm and StudioDell, the former allowing customer insights with valuable feedback and the latter enabling users to share videos on Dell related topics. Dell learned several key points which have subsequently shown their business in a positive light. They learned to listen to customers and also to engage with them and take on board some of their ideas and opinions, some of which influenced new product development decisions. By embracing web 2.0 initiatives, companies can implicitly position themselves within customer centric frameworks focused on the issues of loyalty and conversion amongst customer groups. This is the future for not only business but also the World Wide Web.

The variety of blogs is constantly multiplying. Perhaps the most common is the vlog, which is a blog comprising videos. Others make extensive use of photographs, called a photoblog e.g. Flickr and Instagram. Sites that commonly include text frequently make use of a Content Management System (CMS), rendering it easier to accommodate the file sizes and access to download pictures.

Photoblogging has arisen due to the near ubiquity of the compact digital camera.

Publishing content – immediacy and irrevocability

One of the most recent fashions and something at the heart of the web 2.0 social media revolution is having a company blog. This is now the de facto standard for retaining a two way, on-going relationship with customers and suppliers. A personalised internal view of the organisation through a regularly updated blog can portray the real face of the business and transcend the brand. Care should be taken to reflect existing brand values at the same time to ensure the blog is not perceived as a convenient add-on but rather as an essential communication mechanism delivering value to the reader/contributor.

Importantly the concept of 'content is king' has been surpassed by 'relevant content is king' where customer-focused and user-specific content drives true value. A simple example is the inclusion of a '?' at the end of a blog or social media comment to invite others to post responses, comments and discussions to what previously might have been just a statement. This open engagement and stimulation of online conversation through all channels is at the heart of both web 2.0 and measurable marketing effectiveness.

But remember, once you publish a blog, an email, some news, a website or social media comment, it is immortal and online forever, even if you delete it!

There is a huge upside in publishing digital content. From a humble email to interesting blog, from social media chat to a customer case study every time you publish content online you are allowing your messages to pass far and wide, around the globe and back again, touching customers and prospects on the way.

Authenticity

The issue of authenticity is central to blogging. Marketers and brand managers have to be aware of maintaining credibility before visibility.

Fake or spoof blogs can do great damage to a company's reputation – a famous example of this was "Walmarting across America" in which two Walmart enthusiasts travelled across America reporting on their experiences as they visited Walmarts on their journey.

Whilst the two people did do the journey it emerged that they had been paid to do it by Walmart!

Increasingly there is a case for organisations to hire professional bloggers as part of their marketing team or to outsource this function to an agency. Consider the following statistics (Technorati, 2011):

- 18% of bloggers are professional part- and full-timers
- Corporate bloggers make up 8% of the blogosphere
- 13% of the blogosphere is characterised as entrepreneurs
- There are over 174 million blogs on the internet
- 95% of blogs end up being abandoned

RSS

As well as simply visiting blogs, RSS feeds are an increasingly popular way to access content. An RSS feed allows you to syndicate content. This may be for a favourite topic e.g. news, car racing, etc. This can be done by using an RSS reader application (e.g. RSS Reader) and selecting the type of site feed required.

Remember that your headline is going to decide for 99.9% of people whether they keep reading the post or not.

3.4 Online (or digital) advertising

Advertising is a non-personal form of communication targeted at a mass audience. It is intended to get customers' attention and interest. Specific objectives might include: to raise awareness, increase sales, inform, counter competition, reassure, remind, or to support personal selling.

The key to successful digital advertising, particularly in relation to digital newspapers and magazines, is its ability to bring sound and movement to a traditionally one-dimensional medium. With the decrease in attention spans of 21st century target audiences, coupled with their unwillingness to read off screen for more than an average 400 word count, digital advertising presents brands with an effective way to engage and resonate with target audiences by presenting a fusion of sound, movement, entertainment, insight and information. Digital advertising also allows digital newspapers to offer a multi-media experience to their reader who will often see a 'still' of an advert in the digital paper but by clicking on the picture bring the ad 'to life' as a visual and audio production.

Numerous tools exist for tracking from individual users through to general site traffic ,statistics showing numbers of click-throughs from a particular online advertisement.

There are a wide range of types of digital advertisement, including:

Web banners

A web banner or banner ad is a form of online advert delivered by an ad server usually at the top of a site page. It consists of an advert embedded into a web page, which when clicked will take the user through to the advertiser's website – known as a 'click through'. The results for advertisement campaigns may be monitored in real-time and may be targeted to the viewer's interests, through online behavioural targeting.

Interstitials

An interstitial advert is one which appears after a user has clicked onto a hyperlink but before the user reaches their intended destination. Such interstitial adverts usually have a mechanism for the user to skip the advert, but these are often obscure and hard to locate.

Superstitial

A superstitial is an interactive, non-banner advert that features animation, sound and graphics. It is usually played when the user takes a break in surfing and plays only when fully loaded. This ensures that every user gets a consistent and complete brand message and that each advertiser pays only for guaranteed impressions.

Pop-ups (daughter windows)

Pop-up ads or pop-ups are another form of online advertising, often appearing in a new browser window and usually generated by JavaScript. A variation on the pop-up window is the pop-under advertisement, which opens a new browser window hidden under the active window. This makes it more difficult to determine which website opened them. N.B. Most browsers include features to enable users to block pop-ups and/or filter adverts.

3.5 Affiliate marketing

Affiliate marketing involves third parties in creating a 'closed loop' promotional mechanism. As such it should result in a 'pay per performance' system where a brand owner has to pay commission only when they receive a lead or make a sale. Commission to a referring site is based on the value of the sales or a fixed PPC amount.

Whether or not affiliate marketing is a good investment for marketers depends on a judgement of whether any sales achieved would have been captured anyway, especially in the case of well-known brands.

Aggregators may be comparison sites such as Kelkoo, USwitch or Google Product Search. Each will have different charging models.

Referrers may also be review sites in niche sectors, or 'evaluator intermediaries'.

Anyone can be a useful referrer, and affiliate networks can be built up selectively using market mechanisms created for the purpose such as Commission Junction (http://uk.cj.com).

For more on affiliate marketing, see A4UForum (www.a4uforum.co.uk) and www.comparisonengines.com.

3.6 Podcasting

The term podcast was originally a synthesis of the words 'pod' and 'broadcast'. However, the word podcast has begun to conceptually imply 'Personal On Demand broadcasting'.

Podcasts can be played on any computer, MP3 Player or any digital media portable device. This is distinct from webcasting, which implies a broadcast over the internet usually with a webcam.

Podcasts have a number of advantages: they can be streamed over the internet in real time or they can be downloaded, providing the user the luxury of being able to be listen as required; and the technology to make them is very cheap when compared with traditional radio and television broadcasting. This has meant that small organisations, or indeed anybody with a website, are able to make programmes that can, and in some cases do, reach very large audiences.

Some of the issues a marketer must be aware of when considering implementing podcasting are:

- whether to allow streaming or download
- whether to set up an internet radio station to host to use iTunes
- how to brand your Podcasts and whether to offer multiple channels

Keeping track of your podcast statistics

It is fairly easy to track traffic from your website by being able to record and analyse podcast statistics with Google Analytics, MeasureMap or Mint. But the issue of monitoring downloads, subscriptions and accessing to what degree content has been listened or watched is a slightly different matter as it borders on issues concerning privacy.

- **Feedburner (www.feedburner.google.com)**
  Acquired by Google in 2007, Feedburner organises RSS feeds for you and offers a nice suite of tools to manage and evaluate your traffic.

- **Fruitcast (www.fruitcast.com)**
  Although it is not really a podcast statistic service, it allows you to have advertisements auto-inserted into the beginning or end of your podcasts.

- **Podtrac (http://podtrac.com)**
  This site helps you and your potential advertisers gauge your listenership.

3.7 Mashups

The term 'Mashup' in simple terms refers to data from more than one source integrated into one web application. Its origin stems from the world of music where DJs would mix different genres of music. This then progressed to Video DJs and was then adopted by estate agents who combined property listings from the Craigslist bulletin board with Google Maps, making apartment hunting easier.

Mashups need to be understood as being distinct from simply embedding data from one site in another in order for it to exist as a unified web page. Technically, a mashup web application should consist of three distinct parts: a webpage, a separate entity or content provider (which it accesses using an Application Programme Interface (API) to keep the link dynamic and up to date) and a host. These most commonly, nowadays, are web services offering RSS and other web feeds.

A prime example would be a Hotel website with a map on it to allow guests to find the hotel. But rather than a static picture of a map it is linked dynamically to Google maps to allow guests to plot their route from any direction. Another example is a news website with several RSS feeds appearing on the page from other sources.

Mashup styles

As we deal here only with the less complex side of mashups, marketers need to be aware that it is a continually evolving, complex and multivaried genre. Due to the fact that an API defines and shapes the way an application program may request services from other data sources such as libraries or other operating systems, the issue a marketer should understand is how APIs can assist in business solutions.

Three distinct styles can be deciphered: the first is Web based, which are mashups done in a web browser. The second is Server based and such mashups are done at datacentres or in clouds. Occasionally other services can also be provided. The third and last one is a Data Mashup, where similar types of information and media are combined from multiple sources into a single graphical representation. An example could be AlertMap which combines data from over 200 sources concerning severe weather conditions.

Although on the whole many more user friendly software programmes are appearing on the market, such as Google Mashup Editor, Microsoft Popfly and Mozilla's Ubiquity, there are still central issues that need to be addressed, such as the privacy of data, copyright issues, interoperability and issues as straight forward as downloading times and the quality of data. Service-level agreements are another sore point as they are not always available, but the main drawback is that there is a host of security and regulatory issues that are a persistent source of concern. It is possible that the principles of mashup fuelled by relevant content could form the basis for the next generation of cloud marketing.

3.8 QR Codes

QR Codes (Quick Response Codes) are 2D barcodes that can be scanned by mobile device cameras and then used to direct web browser or application activity to a particular location or to provide a small amount of data to the device. These can be used as part of an off-line marketing campaign to direct users to a particular web page thus providing a rapid call to action.

They have been used in applications as diverse as to providing links to web pages showing ingredient lists for food products, to display hidden information on bus shelter posters.

At present these codes are mainly used for off-line to on-line marketing though the standard was originally designed to allow standard barcode readers to be able to parse the code allowing for the potential of an on-line to off-line transport mode for data, with the QR code being generated then displayed on the mobile device screen.
With many technologies that have remained in the public domain for over a decade there comes a time when it is make or break, or perhaps acceptance that they will always remain in the background or be niche applications. The QR code has now come of age.

3.9 Advergaming

Advergaming, or in-game advertising, is the practice of using video games to advertise a product. With the growth of the internet, advergames have proliferated, often becoming the most visited aspect of brand websites and becoming an integrated part of brand media planning in an increasingly fractured media environment.

Advergames theoretically promote repeated traffic to websites and reinforce brands. Users choosing to register to be eligible for prizes can help marketers collect customer data. Gamers may also invite their friends to participate, which could assist promotion by word of mouth, or 'viral marketing'.

Static advertising within games has been around for a number of years, particularly within sports and racing games where brand signage is commonplace. But only since the massive growth of online gaming and the increased production values within titles, has in-game begun to identify itself as a viable companion to more traditional marketing campaigns.

Historically, advertising within games presented marketers with several obstacles. If brands wanted to get a placement within a game they had to do so during the production process of the title, which meant the negotiation of lengthy lead times. Once the ad was in-game it could not be changed, updated or easily measured.

However, the introduction of dynamic (online enabled) in-game advertising has resulted in a flexible, updateable and creative alternative for marketers looking to access multiple niche audiences.

Marketers can now serve their ads into a game in real time and select the type of game and placement they require. They can even specify the number of impressions that should be served.

Games advertising is one of the most dynamic and fast-growing disciplines within the online landscape. Millions of people in the UK and other countries regularly play games across various platforms for hours on end each week. Uniquely, when we play a game our attention is focused solely on that media because to be distracted is to lose. Consequently 72% of gamers recall ads they have seen for brands in-game (Richards, 2009).

The benefits of in-game advertising
In-game is a unique advertising space that appears to join the dots between, above and below the line marketing. Despite being digital and measurable in a way similar to online and utilising the internet to serve, track and update the ads, it is actually similar in execution and method to TV and outdoor.

Just as internet marketing has evolved from the more basic banner display executions to engage the consumer with an array of clever, interactive and creative formats, in-game marketing is following suit. The gaming ad-networks are moving beyond simply utilising signage efforts such as billboards and are now using 3D objects, in-game video and other media formats that optimise the in-game environment.

The automotive, FMCG, entertainment, male hygiene, sports apparel and wireless/mobile consumer electronics sectors are among those that have recognised what in-game advertising can do to build their brands.

A number of major consumer companies have also employed a gaming expert specifically to work on their in-game presence.

Barriers to growth

There are of course perceived barriers to the kind of growth that online marketing has enjoyed, particularly in the last three years. The IAB has found that in the main, the game players are extremely protective of their passion and more technically knowledgeable than the 'average' consumer. If they disapprove of a commercial presence within their favourite titles they will voice their discontent amongst the widespread gaming community.

In this instance they are very much aware of the imbalance in the advertiser/ consumer relationship - the advertisers need them far more than they need marketing messages within the gaming experience.

There are certain rules to obey for in-game advertising creative. The niche nature of many games' titles offers brands a number of opportunities, but also presents with them restrictions. It is essential that any advertising within a game is relevant to the game in which it appears, therefore not all titles are suitable for such commercial activity. Likewise not all brands suit all games.

Importantly, advertising should not interrupt the game playing experience and marketers need to remember that they are appearing within an entertainment medium and creative executions need to reflect this.

Chapter 4: Social Media

4.1 Introduction

Like it or loathe it, people globally have taken enthusiastically to social networking. It has become an everyday mode of communicating between friends, family and colleagues.

Many businesses are using social media as a core part of their marketing activities.

However, social network marketing has not yet been completely embraced by marketers, especially those in small to medium sized businesses. Time and resource constraints have made people cautious about jumping into the complete unknown. However, as we will see, when implemented as part of an integrated marketing campaign, social network marketing has proven to be very successful.

There is a plethora of social media and social networking sites and, while their key technological features are fairly consistent, the cultures that emerge around them are varied. From geographical segmentation to social interest groups, there is a site for every taste.

Most sites support the maintenance of pre-existing social networks, but others help strangers connect based on shared interests, political views or activities. Some sites cater to diverse audiences, while others attract people based on common language or shared racial, sexual, religious, or nationality-based identities. Sites also vary in the extent to which they incorporate new information and communication tools, such as mobile connectivity, blogging, and photo/video-sharing.

4.2 The growth of social media

Initially the internet (and the websites developed for it) was a very passive medium. Large and small companies would create a variety of content that would then be viewed by consumers. Some of these websites would incorporate some form of retail experience but mostly the consumer would do little more than read. In many ways this was a function of:

- The cost and complexity of creating a website, ensuring that only those companies who could afford to pay for dedicated web designers were able to generate content.
- The mind-set of those organisations. Most of the marketing departments or media companies who developed the initial Web 1.0 sites came from established off-line media or marketing organisations. These teams were used to consumers being passive viewers of content (be it TV or Radio adverts, magazines, newspapers or other adverts.)

This passive, read-only, web had many advantages but also created its own disadvantages:

- **Control of content** – because only substantial organisations could afford to create any meaningful presence the majority of 'real' data was under tight editorial control.

- **Scale** – the number of sites tended to grow proportionately to the number of users on the internet.

This control and scale initially assisted the development and acceptance of the internet. However it quickly became unsustainable for the following reasons:

- **Cost of content creation** – it became increasingly expensive for organisations to have dedicated staff to create and maintain content. As users became more demanding, it was expected that content would be updated on a daily or hourly basis which imposed huge costs on these companies.

- **Lack of revenue** – for the majority of web organisations the business models had assumed a significant penetration into the viewing consumers and venture capital funding had been advanced in the expectation of future income. However companies were finding it hard to capture paying audiences and with the increase in costs were finding the cash 'burn rate' impossible to sustain.

In addition, the huge number of websites in existence, each having extremely small market penetration, made it unattractive for advertisers to purchase advertising further reducing site revenues and stifling growth.

As a result of this financial crisis, developments in technology to enable user generated content were given a huge boost. The key features of these sites are:

- User interactivity
- User generated content
- User growth through peer group invitation and advocacy
- Support of intra-cultural focus

Moving away from the passive viewing model to one where the viewers interact with the content is crucial to the success of Social media (SM) websites. This level of interactivity increases dwell time on the site which leads to increased visibility of site based adverts with a commensurate increase in Click Through Rates and site income. At the most basic level this can simply involve the ability to comment on site content (www.guardian.co.uk) or the inclusion of discussion forums.

Sites have evolved which are almost pure discussion forum based. One of the major forum sites is www.digitalspy.co.uk which, although it contains some editorial content, is used primarily for TV show discussion forums. Once sites move away from users commenting on content to actually making the content the next level of interactivity is reached.

User generated content
This is the holy grail of SM sites – persuading the users to actually create the content for you rather than having to pay for its creation. The first (legal) Social media site in this form was probably www.youtube.com which grew using videos uploaded (and usually created by) the unpaid public wanting to share content with both their own peer groups and the wider public. YouTube is now used heavily by businesses to help promote their own on and off-line material.

The issue of creating and uploading content by the public has clear copyright, defamation and libel issues requiring these Social media sites to employ a range of techniques to protect themselves and their users. This is an additional expense but it would be heavily outweighed by the cost of creating the content in-house. It is estimated that 10 hours of video is uploaded to YouTube every minute; this amount of media creation would be impossible for any organisation to create itself. This level of user created content creates a virtuous circle of an ever-increasing amount of information for users to view, further increasing their dwell time and so increasing the income from the site.

Other user generated content sites include:

1. Blogs (www.blogger.com, http://wordpress.com, www.tumblr.com and www.posterous.com are currently the major blog platforms)
2. Photo upload/sharing sites (flickr, Pinterest and Instagram)
3. Wikis particularly www.wikipedia.com

Peer groups and tribes – invitation and advocacy
Another key defining aspect of social media activity is its growth through Peer Group Invitation and Advocacy. Virtually all the major SM sites use this method as the core of their growth plans and this ties in with the norms of off-line (real world) social interaction where the majority of individuals have a peer group of around 100-150 people (a combination of work colleagues, long term friendships from school/university and local area friendships).

These groupings interleave so that any individual's group is cross-linked into a much wider superset of groupings. Most individuals will have linkages into 3-4 groupings but some will have linkages into up to 15-20 different 'tribes'.

If a social media site captures one of these inter-tribe members then, by persuading them to invite their peer group, the site can gain access to thousands of potential new members at extremely low cost. This peer group invitation is the principle reason why these sites offer to trawl email address lists for invitees.

The advocacy approach is also key. Any new member of a social media site will want to gain an active social circle rapidly to make it worthwhile being a member and investing time in the site. Equally the site will want them to join with other members as quickly as possible to ensure customer retention. Consequently social media sites always provide tools for inviting other members.

Customer retention is a crucial success determinant for all social media sites. Retention (usually measured as the percentage of new users who remain with the site after the first month) varies between 20% and 60% and retention rates of 40% are considered by most venture capital funders to be necessary to capture substantial market share. http://blog.nielsen.com/nielsenwire/online_mobile/twitter-quitterspost-roadblock-to-long-term-growth/.

Note: Peer Group Advocacy is not a phenomenon unique to social media. It was a crucial aspect in the growth of many industries and technologies from fax machines to the early stages of the internet itself. The Economics of Network Industries by OZ Shy is a crucial guide to the growth of such industries and their drivers (Shy, 2001).

Intra-cultural focus leads to increased segmentation
It may seem counter-intuitive but the vast majority of social media sites, most of which will have 10s or 100s of millions of members, consider their members not as an homogeneous mass but instead as collections of 100,000s of individual 'tribes' each with 100-200 members.

This is particularly noticeable within Facebook where only an insignificant percentage of the total membership impinge on any individual's 'wall', and on Google+ which has made the tribal aspect an explicit function of membership, with members defining their contacts in terms of separate 'circles' or tribes.

Within the social media landscape it is potentially easier to identify clear segmentation for a number of reasons:

1. **Membership** – social media websites tend to be associated with 'membership' – this allows the site owner to collect and, potentially, share user demographic information. This information at its most basic level covers age, sex, and geographic location but can also include work location and company, educational level and location. A major element of the site's ability to earn revenue is to target suitable adverts to the users. This membership information is primarily the Launchpad for targeting adverts as significant work is undertaken by site owners to both gauge the CTR of previous adverts and textual analysis of comments and content to select suitable adverts. In addition the most significant indicator of segmentation is:

2. **User group selection** – users rapidly congregate into small tribes of like-minded associates. These associations can be school/work based, interest based, music focused or any of many hundreds of possible, self-created, identifiers. The difference between these associations, and tribes and the formally collected information during the membership process, is that this information is created spontaneously by the members themselves.

This makes this level of demographic information both extremely valuable and also extremely difficult to quantify. It is valuable because the users themselves have chosen to define themselves by these relationships and groupings and so they have a real resonance with the members.

It is difficult to quantify because it is spontaneous and therefore largely random and so is not formally documented within the structure of the site. Within Facebook, these groupings tend to be structured around the 'like' function (particularly related to B2C advertising pages), within Twitter the trending statistics provide a real-time snapshot of what users are currently discussing; with Linkedin they structure around groups.

It is important to note that, unlike real-world tribes, users will not normally be affiliated to a single 'tribe' but will link into a potentially large number of tribes associated with the different aspects of their lifestyle. So they will be in a workmate tribe, a social tribe (which may have multiple cross associations with the work tribe), a hobby tribe (some through probably fewer cross-links), an old friends' tribe (probably associated with previous workmates and/or school) and numerous others such groupings. Some individuals will have intense links with a relatively few groupings whilst others will tend to 'flit' between very many unrelated groups and not have an intensive experience within many groups. Each of these user types has different values to an organisation.

A limited number of intensive users will have considerable power of influence over a relatively few other members/direct friends (first order relationships) and their potential sphere of influence (those people who are friends of their friends (second order relationships) will be limited in scope as there will be substantial overlap within their tribes.

The more 'butterfly' members (who are linked into many groups but are not strongly affiliated to any particular group) may have a weaker influence over their friends but their sphere of influence is potentially greater as there will be much less overlap within their tribes.

This concept of tribes is taken to its extreme in Google+, it is strongly implied within Facebook, has limited effect in Twitter and is currently poorly implemented within media sharing sites – such as YouTube.

How do tribes and user segmentation affect businesses?
The user information explicitly collected by the site owners is a potentially valuable data resource which would enable significant segmentation and analysis of social media but this data is potentially protected by the Data Protection Act and so its use for marketing and marketing analysis is limited.

The implicit information generated by the users has a great deal of value as it has been created by the users who therefore value its existence. However as it is an artefact of the site rather than an element of it (with the exception of Google+ where it has been coded within the site structure) and it is harder to capture and analyse.

The other issue with tribal membership information is that the cost of creation is extremely low and there is little commitment required to join a tribe (there are few initiation rites involved in 'liking' a particular brand or using a hashtag!) or indeed remain a member.

As an example 95,000 people 'like' Stella Artois on Facebook – however this does not imply that they drink significantly more beer than any other group, or indeed would chose Stella over any other beer brand. Equally the fact that a person used the word 'Sofa' in a tweet would not necessarily imply they would wish to follow DFS on Twitter to find out the latest sofa news!

The key lesson from this is that the main beneficiaries of this level of user segmentation and data collection are the site owners and advertisers who wish to market directly through the site using traditional PPC advertising techniques. At present, the ability for non-advertisers to acquire or collate this level of user information is limited – both by the legal constraints of the DPA, the informal structure of the data, and the unwillingness of the site owners to 'give away' a core element of their revenue generation model.

This level of segmentation may seem to add complexity to the development of these sites as it requires the site to have the ability to understand and cater for these inter-member connections, but it offers great benefits:

1. The site can become focused on the needs of different segments rather than being either too generic or exclusive for members.

2. This level of segmentation (particularly the circles approach by Google+) allows advertisers to position their ads correctly targeted, not only at particular user types but also according to the 'mode' they are currently interacting in (for example within a business circle adverts for business services could be highlighted whereas in a social circle other ads might be placed).

3. It reduces 'noise' for the users making the experience much more personal and inviting.

4. It gives the feeling of a private club rather than a huge generic stadium, increasing dwell time and the likelihood of click through to paid content.

These four elements are the core essence of social media. Most sites have some of these elements but relatively few contain all four aspects.

4.3 Opportunities for marketers

With so much to choose from how can we as marketers know how, and where, to start our social networking activity? There is no one site that can cater for all, one place where we can have a social networking presence that can tick all the boxes.

What makes social networking unique to marketers is that it allows individuals, and now organisations, to meet strangers and to make visible their own social networks. The end user is an engaged participant, however, brand engagement is not often an end user's goal.

On most of the larger social networking sites, participants are not necessarily looking to meet organisations, or even new people, but actually communicate with people they already know. Social networking is becoming a communication tool rather than a way of extending social networks.

Sites like LinkedIn encourage the extension of a social network in the true sense of 'networking'. In our own professions, we register on these sites to interact with other marketers for knowledge, ideas and even career progression.

Facebook, Twitter and LinkedIn are in the top 12 visited websites (see Section 4.4) in the world. This growth is giving marketers increased opportunities. Although the understanding of social marketing has increased it is important to remember the core objective is relationship building and not to use them as a sales tool.

With so many platforms available and usage across social media ever increasing it would be easy for marketers to assume that a presence is essential.

Installing your brand on social media is not about choosing one or several social platforms and opening profiles, it is about defining objectives and allocating resources accordingly. The platform choice should be made based on your strategic approach. The social media ecosystem is not a stable one so mass marketing is not a sensible approach. Forgetting geography for a second there are demographics, specialist interest groups and other ways to segment each network's membership.

Competition is something else to monitor, Facebook is by far the most popular social platform but it is also the one where competition is the most intense. If there are much bigger and more successful brands already with a strong presence, does your brand have the resources and compelling strategy that will impact, or are results going to be limited? Think about the return and think about the objectives before jumping on the bandwagon.

A long-term, successful conversation-based engagement platform is a much more ambitious project, which will require more time and energy but can achieve strategic goals, while short-term campaigns may be useful to test the effectiveness of different platforms.

Social networking profiles

Most social networking profiles consist of visible contacts, or 'friends', who must also be users of the same system. A profile is usually generated with typical descriptors such as name, age, location and general interests. Most sites also encourage users to upload a profile photo. Some sites allow users to enhance their profiles by adding multimedia content or adding modules, games and other applications.

The visibility of a profile varies by site and according to user security settings and preferences. By default, profiles on sites such as Friendster and Tribe.net are crawled by search engines, making them visible to anyone regardless of whether or not the viewer has an account. Alternatively, LinkedIn controls what a viewer may see based on whether the user has a paid for account. Sites like MySpace allow users to choose whether they want their profile to be public or private.

Facebook takes a different approach. By default, users who are part of the same 'network' can view each other's profiles, unless a user has decided to deny permission to those in their network. Structural variations around visibility and access are one of the primary ways that social networking sites differentiate themselves from each other and these are particularly evident in recent enhancements to Facebook's privacy settings. Beyond profiles, friends, comments and private messaging, social networking sites vary greatly in features and user base. Flickr is based on photo-sharing; YouTube on video-sharing capabilities; others have built-in blogging and instant messaging technology.

As mobile usage develops there are mobile-specific social networks, for example, Snapchat, but most web-based networks also support limited but growing mobile interactions. Facebook, in particular, now offers advertisers mobile usage on all smart phones.

The 2012 social media Marketing Industry Report investigated how marketers are using social media to grow their business (Stelzner, 2012). The results were very interesting. It shows that:

- The study showed that Marketers still place high value on social media, 83% indicate that social media is important for their business.

- Measurement and targeting are top areas marketers want to master: 40% of all social media marketers want to know how to measure the return on investment (ROI) of social media and find customers and prospects.

- Video marketing holds the top spot for future plans: A significant 76% of Marketers plan on increasing their use of YouTube and video marketing, making it the top area marketers planned to invest in 2012. Similarly, while only 40% of Marketers are using Google+, 70% want to learn more about it and 67% plan on increasing Google+ activities.

- 85% of marketers reported that the number-one benefit of social media marketing is generating more business exposure, followed by 69% believing it was increasing traffic, and thirdly, 65% that social media's number one benefit was providing marketplace insight.

- Facebook, Twitter, LinkedIn, blogs and YouTube were the top five social media tools used by marketers, in that order.

- Social media marketing still takes a lot of time: The majority of marketers (59%) are using social media for 6 hours or more each week, and a third (33%) invest 11 or more hours weekly.

The study also highlighted that social media outsourcing is underutilised. Only 30% of businesses were outsourcing some portion of their social media marketing in 2012, only a slight increase from 28% in 2011.

Advantages (*and constraints*) of social networking
There are five distinct advantages to social network marketing that make it a vital tool to any marketing campaign including:

1. Better targeting – social network marketing can draw a highly targeted segment of internet users to visit a business or website, increasing visibility of content on both a local and global level. *However, there is an increasing number of Social Network sites to monitor only some of which may target your audience.*

2. High return on investment – social network marketing is one of the cheapest ways of marketing currently available providing a high return on investment. Low investment means low risk to even the smallest business. *However, returns on investment need to take into account time and man hours spent as well as money. ROI is not yet proven on many networks.*

3. Does not require specialisation or vast technical skills – most social networking sites are visually oriented and pretty straightforward, which means that practically anyone can use social networking tools. *Again time spent monitoring and adapting needs to be borne in mind as each Network adopts its own methods it becomes a constant learning curve.*

4. Works better than online adverts campaigns – because most internet users are bombarded with adverts every day, as a whole society has become so used to them people are starting to become less receptive to them. Social network marketing provides a personalised view point to attract potential customers to the things that interest them.

Social networking sites, including Facebook, have targeted text advertising with fees aimed at small businesses. LinkedIn's fees can be as low as a few pounds for 1,000 impressions and allow users to set a budget. Advertisers can choose two of seven criteria to target, including geography, industry, seniority and company size.

Social network marketing is not a financial burden but is resource heavy with time being a crucial aspect to a successful campaign.

5. Increased visibility – Social network marketing can help to spread information.

Social media therefore can be used by marketers to help build stronger and deeper relationships, but only if brands identify which platforms work best for them and concentrate their efforts. It constantly comes back to segmentation and targeting. For the long term, the value for marketing on social networking sites may be simply the ability to reach niche groups via advertising on the site and spread information.

The challenge of measuring return on social networking
So, online social networks present an efficient platform for a business to use in the spread of its marketing message. The exposure to advertising on Facebook is clear but does it actually work in gaining sales? Research http://www.tnsdigitallife.com/ claims that social media users were sick of so-called 'digital waste' from brands, with 60% of US and 61% of UK consumers not wanting to engage with them on Facebook or Twitter (TNS Digital Life, 2011).

An important part of any campaign is measurability, and this is no different with social networking activity, which can be measured in the following ways:

- **Homepage adverts** – an example of paid media – adverts that contain creative as well as an option for users to engage with the brand, for example "Become a Fan".

- **Social impressions** – homepage adverts that include social context, like the names of users' friends who are already fans of the brand encouraging a user to follow. This is an example of a hybrid of paid and earned media (see below).

- **Organic impressions –** are social stories that appear on the homepage of friends of users who have engaged with a brand or become a fan of that brand.

- **Earned media –** is the term being used to describe brand mentions on Facebook that are broadcasted, or shared, by a consumer, whereas organic impressions offer a more controlled way to generate earned media from paid advertisements.

Rule of thirds

Striking the right balance in your daily dose of social networking can be a tricky thing to find. But following the Rule of Thirds may take you beyond the idea of social media as a distraction.

When socially networking online you should communicate:

- **One third about YOU –** what you are up to, what you are thinking, what you are not liking, what you are seeing and how you are feeling.

- **One third about SIGNPOSTING –** sharing with others what you have seen in your online travels from favourite videos, images, news clips and blogs.

- **One third about the SELL –** your products and services if you are an organisation, or what you want your friend or colleague to do as a result of listening to you.

Many sectors, organisations and industries are experiencing clarity and effective communications by choreographing their online content in this way, applying it to newsletters, blogs, social media and customer engagement.

The future for social networking?

Social networking is here to stay and must be integrated into your digital strategy. Like all marketing projects, measurement and control is essential so that we are always learning from what we are doing.

Marketers must question whether social media is all about numbers and 'likes', or whether an integration of objectives with longer-term strategy will bring true return on investment.

It is an easy assumption to make that Facebook's continued rise to global dominance means that it is now becoming a one-stop-shop to global social media marketing. But when we remember the ethos and values of the marketing discipline as a whole, then we must ask ourselves if Facebook is the right platform to truly engage with stakeholders, and does its coverage really provide value for your brand? This is a question that each marketer must answer for themselves.

4.4 Key social media businesses

The social media sector is characterised by a relatively large number of small players and a small number of extremely large organisations. The major players are: Blog Providers (see Chapter 3); Facebook; LinkedIn and Twitter.

Top visited websites globally according to Alexa rankings, as of September 2013 (Alexa, 2013):

1. Google
2. Facebook
3. YouTube
4. Yahoo!
5. Baidu.com
6. Wikipedia
7. QQ.com
8. Amazon
9. Windows Live
10. Linkedin
11. Twitter
12. Blogspot

However, the list does not include those much hyped sites like Pinterest, Yammer, Stumble, Instagram, Flickr, etc. which feature in many discussions of Social Media but as their non-listing shows they are niche.

Cavazza has for four years produced an interesting infographic on the social media landscape (Cavazza, 2013). His 2013 version (See Figure 4.1) shows how Facebook, Twitter and Google+ are the core central networks due to their mass appeal and large amount of functionality but there are peripheral groups of smaller players that hold niche specialisms based on interest, interactivity and media platform.

Figure 4.1 Social Media Landscape 2013 (Cavazza, 2013)

Although Cavazza's graph is useful for understanding the complexity of social media, it is not an exhaustive list of available services. For example, one of the reasons Facebook should not be considered as a one-stop-shop for social marketing is that it has a lack of presence in Russia and Asia. Cavazza's graph also only reflects western countries' social platforms; it does not take into account eastern markets like Russia, or Asian markets like China or Japan.

Another blogger, Vincenzo Cosenza, annually produces a world map of social networks and this gives a nice visual of the coverage that the largest social networks have globally. In the past year the main development has been the contraction from 17 different top social networks to just 6. Facebook is dominant but not totally ubiquitous, with V Kontakte being the major player in Russia and Qzone (QQ.com) in China http://vincos.it/world-map-of-social-networks/.

Facebook
Facebook is by far the largest and most comprehensive social media site in existence today with over 1 billion users. The growth of Facebook over recent years (Facebook was only opened to the public in 2006), and the developments it has faced are documented exhaustively and a useful starting point is http://en.wikipedia.org/wiki/Facebook. The key benefit Facebook has over its competitors (MySpace, Bebo and FriendsReunited) is its combination of scale, ease of use and willingness to allow third party application developers to create content (everything from Scrabble to Farming) which further increases dwell time on the site and increases revenue.

Businesses are now beginning to use Facebook to advertise themselves, and the number of businesses creating Facebook pages is increasing exponentially. At present it is hard to gauge the financial benefit of this activity as the majority of these pages do not offer substantial interactivity other than the offering of discount vouchers, etc.

The other concern is the lack of commitment on the part of the consumer (the majority of this activity is B2C) as the only requirement is for the user to 'like' the business and so follow its content. This one-click activity is easy to do yet does not normally engender significant commitment.

Facebook has not lost sight of the need to evolve. After acquiring mobile photo sharing application, Instagram with its 35 million users, for $1 billion, Facebook bought another mobile start-up called Glancee underscoring the importance of mobile to its growth strategy.

Twitter

Twitter has quickly garnered 500 million users, though only 200 million seems to be active. The service has attracted huge media attention in the five years of its existence and is one of the fastest growing social media sites at present. Sidebar ads are explicitly not included but 'promoted tweets' are one key source of revenue.

One aspect that has enabled its huge growth is the willingness of Twitter.com to allow third parties to create separate interfaces not only for businesses to monitor and manage their presence but also for users. (Tweetdeck was one of these third party Apps that has since been integrated into the core Twitter platform.)

The other unique selling point of twitter has been its native integration into the mobile arena. Twitter, with its 140 character limit – the same as SMS – has a much closer relationship with mobiles and with its intentionally simple interface and willingness to allow third party applications. This has resulted in an explosive growth in the number of mobile interfaces to Twitter with the result that 46% of Twitter users will use their mobile to tweet and 40-45% of all tweets originate on a mobile. This has significant implications for the future of mobile marketing.

The 'limitation' of 140 character messages and the ability to use either a laptop or smartphone has created the phenomenon of TV tweeting with TV viewers tweeting their comments during the show (the simple interface and quickness of use contribute to this dynamic function).

Twitter has also been used for:

1. Protests – protests have been extensively commented on live by people involved in marches and demonstrations worldwide.

2. Policing – police have used Twitter to share information both within the police force and with the public.

3. News Reporting – the rapid reaction times of Twitter have meant that it is frequently the first (albeit sometimes unreliable) reporter of news events from earthquakes to the death of Michael Jackson.

4. Space Exploration – the open API has allowed NASA and other organisations to automate tweets from rockets, space shuttles and space probes.

For marketers, it is still very much a relationship tool, and can be used to engage in debate, encourage focus on niche topics, raise awareness of marketing initiatives (trade shows, new products, etc.). However, too much heavy promotion will not be tolerated.

The short time frame of tweets and twitterers' attention means it is especially suitable for messages with a strong topical element. Twinings Tea used a spell of hot weather to suggest that its followers brewed a cup of refreshing tea! They also invited feedback on new tea flavours.

Twitter users are influenced more by friends. 69% of users will follow based on recommendations by friends, with 47% based on online search, 44% based on Twitter suggestions, and only 31% based on promotions.

LinkedIn

LinkedIn is the most popular network to build and maintain business contacts for marketers. Think of it as your online resumé and that of your organisation.

Groups provide a forum for the discussion of specific topics e.g. digital marketing! These can also be branded, providing another focal point for the activities of an organisation and allow users to punch above their weight.

As of September 2013, LinkedIn reports more than 238 million acquired users in more than 200 countries and territories (LinkedIn, 2013).

One of the key mistakes that people make when trying to overtly self-promote or increase the profile of their business or brand is to jump straight in and use the power of research and targeting to send unsolicited sales messages to communities, groups and individuals. But this is not what LinkedIn was designed for, and the same is true for other social media in the digital marketing mix. It is a collaborative and networking community, a platform for sharing ideas, thoughts and opinions. Something like a business networking breakfast from the comfort of your desk or sofa. And therein lies a potential frustration. Just how much can you and should you overtly 'sell' on a business social networking platform?

The general principle is to not think of or use the words 'sell' or 'sales' when you are thinking about LinkedIn or social media. It may be part of your digital hub and it may create enquiries and leads that could be an eventual outcome (and many are generating excellent high quality business leads from it). But far better and safer to use and think strategically about words like 'influence', 'sharing', 'intelligence', 'collaboration'. These are words much more akin to the attitudes and thought patterns of others when they are using LinkedIn. That is the mindset they are in when they are there so it is best to communicate with them at that time on their terms and in a style appropriate to how they are feeling. Help customers to buy rather than try to sell.

- **Research** – find groups of like-minded individuals, focused around your interests, products and market sector.

- **Listen** – listen to the discussion threads, listen to comments and the atmosphere inside debates that interest you.

- **Contribute** – add value to the debate, comment positively and sometimes critically, stimulate others to comment back.

- **Lead** – start new discussions, pose interesting new angles to old stories.

- **Give** – provide links to resources, videos, training, tutorials and informative blogs, share and share alike.

Build your credibility, your value and your presence before beginning to ask for leads, business or using overt promotion. Build a following and professional standing on LinkedIn before you even consider the word 'sales' and you will be surprised just how receptive others will be to what you say in the future.

Victoria Ipri, who offers LinkedIn consulting, provides these tips for marketers looking to exploit LinkedIn:

1. Groups that are similar to you are your competitors and you will not get any business by just connecting with them. You want to join groups that are similar to you so that you can network and participate in discussion panels, but you do not want those groups to be your only connections because essentially they are your competitors.

2. The main goal is to not stick with the pack because there is no business within the pack.

3. Just because LinkedIn allows you to join 50 groups does not mean you should. You cannot actively participate in 50 groups, eight to ten is plenty.

4. Always write your summary in first person, not in third person. Write it like you are speaking directly to your readers.

5. Always include your contact information. Most people say they want to be contacted, but a lot of people do not tell people how to contact them. They leave no contact information. A lot of this is fear, but this is pointless because your contact information is probably already accessible through a quick Google search.

6. When choosing a headline, use words that are relevant to your skills, and words people would use to search for you.
E.g. http://www.linkedin.com/in/victoriaipri

Google+
Google+ was launched in July 2011 and according to its own statistics is the fastest growing social network. Despite being branded a failure by large portions of the media, Google+ grew in terms of active usage to 343 million users by May 2013 to become the second most used social platform after Facebook.

However, data from Nielsen Media Research revealed that in March 2013 the average US Google+ user spent a mere 6 minutes and 47 seconds on the site, compared to more than 6 hours spent on Facebook (Graziano, 2013). As a result, it has not been able to win over brands and businesses which have instead turned to connect with customers on competing websites.

Nevertheless, many companies are present on Google+ because of the importance Google, as a search engine, places on presence.

4.5 Social bookmarking
As with many of the most popular areas of the web, social bookmarking has its roots in academia where educators and learners shared data with others.

With the benefits of 'sharing' now commonplace in social networking, social bookmarking allows users to share quickly and easily, lists and bookmarks on particular topics. Using tags or keywords the social bookmarker is able to add a website to lists of similar and relevant sites. Unlike file sharing the actual resources themselves are not shared, just the bookmarks and tags that link to them. In this way it is a highly efficient and an easily accessible use of internet linking.

Why is it important?

Social bookmarking essentially has two purposes. For the website owner it is a highly efficient way of creating backlinks and traffic to a particular website. Because the link is content-specific, each tag and keyword for it should be able to attract highly targeted visitors so quality of website visitors, if done correctly, should be high.

For the consumer it is a highly efficient way of keeping in touch with particular subjects of interest. By subscribing to the RSS feed of the bookmark site they are able to keep in constant touch with the addition of new tags and items on the list.

This sharing is inherent and crucial to the effectiveness and popularity of social media websites.
This is also a fundamental difference between social bookmarking and search engines which typically rely on non-human algorithms often losing the context of the resource.

Social bookmarking has proven mainly to be useful for US based marketers in the technology sector, enabling them to stimulate interest and discussion on particular niche topics. Social bookmarking sites include:

- www.Pinterest.com – 85 million users

- www.reddit.com – 16 million users

- www.stumbleupon.com – 15 million users

- www.delicious.com – 5.5 million users

- www.tweetmeme.com – 5.4 million users

- www.digg.com – 4 million users

(ebiz MBA, 2013)

Of all of the available social bookmarking sites a growing favourite is www.Scoop.it where you can curate rich content, with links to a host of multi media resources, articles, web pages and videos.

4.6 Word of mouth (WOM) and viral marketing

WOM is not a new concept. It refers to any interpersonal communications which the receiver views as impartial. In essence it is as simple as a colleague coming into work and telling the team that the film they saw last night was excellent and well worth going to see. But WOM can be positive or negative. Indeed the challenge for the marketer is two-fold: how to manage and capitalise on positive WOM and how to minimise negative WOM.

The term 'Viral Marketing' was first coined in 1997 by Steve Jurvetson and Tim Draper. Since its introduction, it has become synonymous for a an amplified version of word of mouth. Viral marketing can be defined as making e-mail into a form of advocacy or word of mouth referral endorsement from one client to other prospective clients.

It is important to note that WOM still exists independently of the internet. Viral marketing has developed in an unplanned fashion predominantly through the use of e-mail due to its simplicity, ubiquity and because the communication is free and requires no particular effort by the sender, unlike traditional postal mail or telephone.

Viral marketing now encompasses a number of technologies including SMS (Text) messages, videos, multimedia messages, and Bluetooth transfers between mobile devices.

Marketers can benefit from the low cost and potentially wide reach of viral messaging. However a key hurdle is finding a subject that is humorous/fascinating/controversial enough to be worth recipients passing it on. It is not possible to design a 'Viral Campaign' they just happen.

Tippex's 'Hunter Shoots a Bear' is a good example of a B2B viral campaign aimed at (bored) stationery buyers in their offices (Tippexperience, 2013).

Chapter 5: Mobile

5.1 The growth of mobile and mobile technology

It is not only the desktop that provides Digital marketers with
opportunities. Mobile communications and particularly the explosive
growth in Smart phones have brought the mobile device to the forefront
of innovative marketing. The term M-commerce is not yet common but
is likely to become so, as the mobile device becomes the main channel
of communications in the future. Mobile devices have two unique
advantages for marketers: they are personal to the user and they are
always on. So we are no longer addressing a desk top or laptop device
which could be being used by multiple people and often turned off. We
now have the potential to talk to the individual 24/7. For some
consumers their (smart) mobiles are umbilicaly tied to them, they take
them everywhere and many take them to bed! The Smartphone sits at
the centre of our lives at home and at work, and so is key the
integration of a customer journey.

Mobile communications media

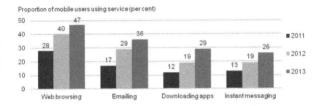

**Figure 5.1 Use of mobile data services among mobile users
(Ofcom, 2013)**

Hardware types

Mobile marketing can be implemented over a variety of different types
of hardware. For each one you should bear in mind the key user
restrictions so that marketing communications can be tailored
accordingly to enhance the consumer experience.

Basic mobile phones (still the majority of installed phones) – can make voice calls, and send and receive SMS messages. Whilst the benefit for the marketer is the high degree of penetration, thought needs to be given to the small screen size, lack of internet connectivity and basic numeric keypad for prospects to enter their responses.

Smartphones (now the majority of phone purchases) i.e. mobile phones that offer advanced capabilities, such as allowing users to download applications to their phones, geolocation (GPS), touchscreens and which run on fully-featured mobile operating systems such as Apple iOS and Android. They usually have a QWERTY keyboard and allow wireless internet connectivity via either 3G or Wi-Fi. Marketers should consider that whilst smartphones have bigger screens and keyboards than basic phones, the screens are still considerably smaller than on PCs/ laptops and the small QWERTY keyboards can be fiddly to use, so communications should be kept as simple as possible with straightforward response mechanisms.

Tablet computers – (e.g. Apple iPad, Samsung Galaxy, Blackberry Playbook, etc.). Offering a cut down desk-top experience, with limitation on some functionality and viewing limitations. (Notably, iPad does not play Adobe flash). Also, whilst growing in popularity, these devices are by no means ubiquitous and tend to vary in operating systems and screen sizes. Nevertheless it is predicted that Tablet sales will have overtaken PC sales in 2013.

E-readers – (e.g. Amazon Kindle, Sony) These are highly portable, lightweight devices with screen sizes similar to tablets, although their primary purpose is for reading digital books and publications.They often have Wi-Fi capability, but 3G functionality is less widespread. Due to their primary purpose as digital publication readers, users may be less willing to respond to peripheral marketing communications, and may not be able to receive such communications when away from the home.

The mobile landscape is constantly evolving. New Smart devices with easy to use software and creative tariffs from the network operators are encouraging people of all ages to use more of their functionality from music, video and pictures to email communications and GPS mapping on the move. The mobile phone has evolved far beyond simple voice and text messaging.

Players in mobile marketing

Marketers entering into mobile marketing must be aware of the roles played by different parties in the overall mobile marketing ecosystem. In order to plan mobile marketing activities effectively, marketers must be aware of the different aims and objectives and areas of responsibility of those parties who will affect the success of any mobile marketing activity.

The main players to be aware of are as follows:

- **Service providers – (for example O2, Orange, Vodafone).** These mobile phone networks have considerable power, in particular they will have detailed guidelines on the types of communications and messaging that companies can engage in with their customers, and it is advisable to be aware of these before engaging in any marketing activity. This is a sensitive area as essentially it is the service providers' customers who will comprise the customer segments for SMS/MMS mobile marketing activity, so of course the service providers will be extremely careful not to annoy/offend their customers via third party mobile marketing. It is also worth bearing in mind that the service providers already have close ties with the handset manufacturers, so it is worth utilising these existing relationships at the start of marketing planning.

- **Operating system owners – for example, Apple iOS, Microsoft Windows Phone, Google Android**. Operating system owners need to be included in any initial planning activity, since differing operating systems necessarily have differing technical and operational restrictions, as well as restrictions from a branding perspective.

- **App designers/developers –** these may range from 'one man bands' all the way through to large companies such as Microsoft and Apple. For App development, they need to be made aware of the technical/brand guidelines and restrictions imposed by the handset suppliers and service providers so that they can design functional and appealing Apps that are in line with branding requirements and the technical specifications of the network and the handset.

- **Media owners and ad networks –** these companies are usually dealt with by media agencies, acting for the advertiser, although they can be directly engaged with as well. The media agency/advertiser needs to ensure that the media owners are fully briefed about the media requirements, again bearing in mind any restrictions imposed. Some media owners such as Apple place high threshold budgets for a campaign i.e. U$100,000 for an iAd campaign.

  Mobile payment providers – for example PayPal, M-Pesa. Due to the public nature of mobiles, where the campaign involves payments being taken over a mobile device, you should ensure that the payment provider is involved in the initial planning discussions. There can often be questions to resolve about the terms of the payment and these need to be communicated to the advertiser and agencies so that this can be made explicit in any marketing communications.

The market for generic web access is currently constrained by the small screen size of phones and/or limited support for some web technologies such as flash. Relatively low bandwidth access is also a constraint.

Historically some sites were created as dedicated mobile microsites which offer the majority of the content of the core site but with simplified layout, graphics and technology to enable mobile browsers to access the site cleanly and over lower bandwidth connections.
This leads to the complexity of needing to support two different access mechanisms and analyse the data separately.

A more prominent approach now is to adopt a Responsive web design that adjusts the layout of the site according to the size of the screen on the device often pushing the navigation tools down below the main page content.

One interesting aspect of the growth of mobile access is **Location Based Marketing.** Many mobile devices now have GPS features allowing them to be aware of (and report on) their location. This has been used to a limited degree in some geo-sensitive services such as FourSquare and Facebook Places. In the future services will use this location data to target advertisements (such as discount vouchers when the consumer is near a coffee shop). The proximity of the customer (in both time and place) reduces the time between the marketing and the resultant action enabling much quicker, more effective analysis of the results.

Mobile marketing
Increasingly the mobile is becoming the tool by which to access and engage with consumers. Consumer brands such as Coca Cola, Nokia and MTV are producing customised campaigns specifically for this medium. The growth of more efficient technology, such as increases in coverage, bandwidth and capacity at cost effective prices has renewed consumer awareness and nearly all phones now come ready configured to work with Multimedia Messaging Service (MMS).

5.2 Mobile advertising
Mobile Advertising display formats
There are several types of mobile display advertising that the mobile marketer needs to be aware of – each of which has particular specific strengths.

The mobile marketer needs to be aware of when and where to deploy these effectively. As users feel a very personal affinity to their mobile phones there is considerable opportunity to annoy prospects with inappropriate or ill-timed communications.

The main types of mobile display ads are as follows:

- **Mobile banner ads** – these are horizontal online ads usually found either across the top or bottom of a mobile device screen in a fixed placement. These ads are particularly suited to raising awareness within the mobile environment, but in order to do this effectively it is crucial to undertake customer research and analysis beforehand to ensure your ads are being placed on sites and Apps which are relevant to your key customer segments. Banner ads can also be used with a 'call to action' to either gain leads or sales transactions. However, in order for this approach to work effectively, not only do the ads need to be positioned in relevant sites, but they need to be very concise, with impactful creative and a clear benefit for the prospect. Even better if the promotion is time-restricted to encourage an immediate response.

- **Interstitials** – this is a web page not requested by a user, containing an advertisement that often opens in a new browser window when the user has clicked on a link within the current page. They can also appear within MMS messages sent to the user. These type of ads need to be used very carefully as there is a high potential of irritating the end user, since they do not ask to see these ads, and it can slow down the task they are trying to achieve – with speed of achieving tasks being particularly important to users when using the mobile internet out of the home. Mobile marketers must therefore always check when considering these types of ads that the content that will be displayed offers value to the user: be that relevant information, or entertainment since these ads can be easily dismissed, with the knock-on effect of damaging the advertiser's reputation for responsible customer-focused communications.

- **In-app ads** – these ads can be extremely effective as long as the advertiser has taken the time to understand the customer profiles of those using the App, and is offering valued content relevant to their needs.

  As long as this vital planning step has been undertaken, in-App ads offer advertisers an audience who are already engaged with using the App – if the advertiser is offering a similar or related service, there is a high chance this will appeal to the current App user-base. App users however are particularly time/task focused (often the purpose of Apps is to achieve certain tasks quicker and more easily than using their related websites), so advertisers need be sure that their offering demonstrates clear value. For example a restaurant review service could advertise on a location-services App when users search for 'restaurants'. Always be aware that many users will pay money for ad-free versions of Apps – which underlines the importance of creating engaging ads that clearly demonstrate real customer value.

- **Mobile video ads** – using 3G technology, it is possible to transmit video ads, which are growing rapidly in popularity on the 'fixed' internet due to their greater impact and engagement with their target customers. However, 3G technology still has bandwidth restrictions which mean that long video ads will often require 'buffering' which negates the creative impact of the ad. If mobile video ads are to be used, it is crucial that the creative production agency design the content specifically for use with 3G (rather than just repurposing 'fixed' internet banner ads), and test it thoroughly before presenting back to the client. In addition, the creative needs to take into account the screen size, banner unit size and the screen resolution to ensure any video is clear and simple to follow.

Mobile v traditional adverts

It is important to understand where mobile communications fit into the overall communication mix – what their advantages are over more traditional forms of advertising and when they can be integrated effectively with other forms of advertising.

The main advantages of mobile advertising are:

Build awareness – mobile banner ads can be a good way to build awareness of related services that may be of interest to users. For example individual restaurants advertising on a restaurant booking App or mobile website. This should be looked at in the light of the overall communications mix, so should be reinforced via other relevant communication media, both online and offline, e.g. print ads in local newspapers, online pay per click ads, etc.

Transactions and revenue generation – in addition to generating awareness, mobile ads can also be used to generate a 'call to action' and hence generate revenue. Using the restaurant example above, a mobile ad could feature a time-limited offer for a restaurant near to the user's location – thus generating a highly relevant and timely offer that may well result in a transaction.

Start a conversation – mobile has the advantage that it can be used to start a conversation and continue engagement through short, relevant micro messages, for example micro-blogs on a brand's Facebook site or short Twitter feeds asking for a response. In order to generate meaningful response rates, the brand needs to have a pre-existing relationship with the user, whereby the user has expressed an interest in the brand and is open to receiving more communications. Unsolicited SMS messages from brands are not viewed positively by mobile users.

Crowd-sourcing ideas – taking the point above, this can be expanded further to use these conversations to open up questions and tap into the creativity of their users, and to harness the democracy and immediacy of the mobile medium to suggest new developments and services they would find useful.

Market feedback and service improvements – similar to the point above, the mobile medium can be used to ask for either general or very specific feedback. It is especially useful where it is requested immediately after the user has just used the service so it is still uppermost in their mind. Also, higher responses can be generated from feedback requests that appear very quick and easy to complete.

Lead generation – mobile communications can be used to get users to register their interest in a brand, so that they can be followed up later with relevant information. An example would be a car brand advertising on a route-planning website, with the 'call to action' of the ad asking for users to register their email address, so that the brand can send more information/ personalised offers. This could be integrated with more traditional PC banner ads, as well as offline ads such as print ads in magazines.

Engagement and retention – once these prospects have converted into customers, then mobile is an excellent medium for building customer engagement and retention. Customers can be asked to register their particular areas of interest at the outset of the relationship, and can then be sent regular, timely offers personalised to their own particular requirements. For example a travel agent offering cheap flights to a particular destination at particular times of the year via SMS messaging, or a coffee shop texting daily offers to commuters at 6am each morning. Similarly, by sending vouchers/ coupons that can be shown in store on their mobile, this extra convenience saves the customer having to remember to print out the voucher and bring it with them.

Competitions and rewards – these are another valuable engagement tool. Again, the immediacy of the mobile medium makes them more powerful. For example rewards/ loyalty points that can be redeemed in store direct from the mobile device. Competitions can work well in combination with offline media: for example printed scratch-cards which reveal barcodes on winning cards that can be scanned for instant wins which can be redeemed against either online or offline purchases.

Create personalised brand experience/one-to-one communication – mobile has the ability to provide very relevant and personalised communications, but it does depend on the brand capturing upfront the individual requirements and preferences of opted-in users.

For example if a customer opted-in to receive communications from a family restaurant chain and provided information of how many children they had, where their nearest restaurant was, and what days and times of the day they were most likely to visit, then very timely and relevant offers could be sent to them to use on the same day. In this way it can be seen that the relevance of the communications is dependent on the amount of information that the customer wishes to submit (in addition to the transactional information gathered) – so you need to ensure that privacy policies are communicated upfront, as well as the benefits of opting-in.

Cost effective – by using mobile media such as Twitter feeds and Facebook page updates, timely information can be communicated very quickly and effectively, and at a very low cost, as can promotional emails (to opted-in prospects) which have been optimised to read well on mobile devices. These enjoy the same cost savings as more traditional digital media, whilst also having the advantage of greater immediacy as these messages can be picked up when users are out and about, and even checked for latest offers when prospects are in store. In contrast, using more traditional offline media such as direct mail and magazine advertising can be expensive and are relatively much slower to produce, so that offers may have been made uncompetitive by competitor activity by the time the messages are received by prospects.

5.3 Apps

As a deliverer of a product or service the App has caught a lot of imagination for marketers. As a method of communication there are problems with the sheer volume of Apps now available. There are over 750,000 Apps on each of the iTunes and Google Play stores. Over 50 billion Apps have been downloaded since 2007 from the ITunes store and a similar number from the Android store. (97% of which are free). Consequently any new App now requires a communications campaign in its own right through other media to raise awareness of its launch.

Chapter 6: Digital Marketing Campaigns
6.1 Getting started

Planning a digital marketing campaign is not dissimilar for the most part from planning any other marketing campaign. In many ways, the internet and associated technologies have simply added more tools to the marketing mix. As usual we need to start by setting objectives.

1. Target Audience – a critical starting point is to define exactly who you are talking to. Who is your key audience in the campaign and which other customer segments might benefit from hearing your messages too?

2. Objectives – you cannot run an effective campaign without establishing your targets at the outset. What are your strategic targets, the ones that will help you to deliver your bigger organisational goals? What key performance indicators are you going to use so you can monitor how the campaign is progressing and check the success at the end?

3. Messages – what is the lead message or proposition for this campaign? What back up messages will support the lead message? Are these consistent with other campaigns you have run or are running and consistent with your brand?

4. Creative – what electronic and printed materials do you need for your campaign? Have you factored the cost of producing and delivering these into your campaign plan? The costs of these need to be included in your objectives because if you over spend the profitability of your campaign will reduce.

5. Channels – how will your target audience experience your campaign? Where will they see, hear and sample it? Think both traditional channels like PR, advertising and direct mail as well as electronic channels such as web, email and social media. Join all your delivery channels together in a nice simple visual so everyone knows where your campaign is happening and what is expected as an outcome from each element.

6. Timing – everything at each step needs to be time bound so set some realistic yet challenging timescales for each element. Identify your start date and target end date but remember to build in a review stage so you can analyse and learn from the outcomes and results of your campaign.

6.2 Campaign planning framework

In order to plan your campaign it is useful to use a framework such as PR Smith's SOSTAC® Planning System (Smith, 2011). Reproduced with kind permission of PR Smith. SOSTAC® is a registered trademark of PR Smith, www.prsmith.org. This stands for:

- Situation
- Objectives
- Strategy
- Tactics
- Actions
- Control

Situation

The first stage is to assess your current situation. The sorts of questions you need to consider include:

- How are customers using new digital media to discover, select and purchase products and services?
- What devices do customers now have?
- How will they find new products – maybe through search engines, social media such as social bookmarking or discussion groups?
- What information do you have about their usage of online media?
- What do you do about those prospects who are not online or receptive to online promotion?
- How have the competitive forces changed with the internet? Are there new entrants, perhaps from other countries?

Objectives

Having assessed where you are now the next stage is to set your objectives for where you want to be.

In digital marketing a useful model for considering objectives is the 'five Ss', developed by PR Smith:

- Sell – use the internet as a sales tool
- Serve – use the internet as a customer service tool
- Speak – use the internet as a communications tool
- Save – use the internet for cost reduction
- Sizzle – use the internet as a branding tool

(Smith, 2011)

Using a framework such as this, you can identify specific objectives which will exploit the digital potential. For example for 'Save', you might think of reducing your costs or those of your customer by using online transactions, enquiries, downloadable resources, etc.

Typical detailed objectives for a website might include: online revenue, enquiries, page impressions, repeat visitors, downloads, sign-ups (e.g. to newsletters), churn rates and so on.

Strategy

Strategic considerations will include:

- Identifying and prioritising target markets
- Developing the online value proposition (OVP)
- How far can the organisation move towards an 'e-business' model, where a large part of its business processes are linked to its online presence?
- What integration of back office, databases, web front end, etc. would be required? This is sometimes called the ratio of 'bricks and clicks'
- How will the brand transfer online?

Tactics

This for many people is the exciting part! What digital tools are you going to deploy? What new approaches can you take to exploit the latest technological advances?

While accepting that any integrated marketing communications campaign should ideally contain an element of both offline and online tactics in order to engage and resonate with the target audience(s), digital communications do provide several distinct advantages including cost, creativity, speed and flexibility. It is vital as part of this process to think about digital marketing as a balance between short term and long term; tactical and strategic. But even with the short term it may not be as effective in directly generating sales in a commercial environment as the rest of the organisation might like to believe. Setting reasonable expectations about what each media will deliver is a key element in setting the boundaries and prioritising the most effective way forward.

It may well be that the organisation has inadequate internal resources to carry out its plans, and will need to involve external specialist suppliers such as web designers, PR consultants, affiliate marketing specialists and so on.

Deployment of the various tools and resources needs to be carefully planned so they work together and in the right sequence. It is no use sending a compelling e-mail shot to your prospects if the landing page on the website is not ready, or if the product is not yet available. Since many people will probably be involved in a campaign, you need to co-ordinate their actions and ensure they have the resources (people, money, materials) to carry out the plan.

Actions

Having done your planning, set your strategy and identified your tactics you then need action. Drawing up a specific action plan with identified responsibilities for delivery, costs and timescales is essential.

Typical e-marketing actions might include:

- Creation and launch of a new website
- Creation and execution of a staged e-mail campaign
- Follow up with a postal or mobile campaign
- Capture of prospect data for use in a customer relationship management (CRM) database
- Implementation of a viral marketing campaign
- Analysis of website analytics to measure success

Control

Fortunately the internet provides marketers with unprecedented monitoring capabilities in the form of website analytics (see Chapter 7), e-mail open and click-through rates, responses to online promotions and so on. These are essential to set up and to monitor throughout the campaign, but even more important are the metrics which relate to achieving the objectives directly.

For example, have we achieved the conversion-to-sales rates hoped for? What effect has our campaign had on customer loyalty? How has our reputation changed? Have we improved our financial ratios? Early and perhaps continuous measurement of the key metrics is the most likely way to be successful in achieving your objectives.

Chapter 7: Measuring Digital Marketing
7.1 The purpose of online measurement

"Half the money I spend on advertising is wasted; the trouble is I don't know which half."

This quote is often attributed to Lord Leverhulme (of soap powder fame) and is much quoted both to justify increasing market spend and as a stick to beat marketing. Certainly it is well known that much marketing effort produces unknown and unmeasurable results - making marketing more of an art than a science.

The purpose of measurement for digital campaigns is the same as the purpose of measuring more traditional forms of marketing. It is to:

1. Measure marketing productivity
2. Examine return on marketing investment (ROMI)
3. Evaluate customer satisfaction and involvement
4. Measure market share and forecast demand

The majority of problems in measuring offline marketing success stem from the lack of immediacy between the marketing activity and the action, and also from the inability to directly and cost-effectively collect, collate and interpret any link between the activity and the action. In many cases the key problem is the cost of collecting suitable data. Additionally the vast majority of organisations will be running more than one marketing activity at a time and so any increase in enquiry, footfall, or sales could be attributed to any or all of these activities.

Ideally, in order to separate the effects of each marketing activity a business would have only one activity at a time, then collect the results and assess the effectiveness. In the offline world this is clearly impossible but on the internet it might be achievable, as with effective tracking and analysis it can separate the effects of different simultaneous campaigns.

Marketing multiplier – moving on from vanity metrics

The easiest things to measure are often irrelevant. We call these 'vanity metrics': visitors to your website, the number of Twitter followers, impressions on a Facebook posting, the circulation figures for a magazine in which you have an article... the list goes on.

Why are these things pointless? Because less might be more. If the numbers are large they are likely to include people who have no real interest in you, your products and services. The recent publicity over 'Like' farms in India and agencies where one can buy Twitter followers points to the hollowness of some metrics.

Awareness is pointless if it does not result in a positive sentiment, action or a 'sale'. A Marketing Multiplier gets you thinking about the real deal, the places where you can make a difference to your highest priority customers, the ones who will help you deliver proper value and return on investment.

It is all about your customer journey along the Sales Funnel: the step-by-step process along which you are guiding your customer in your communications. The trick is to measure the effectiveness of each and every communication point in terms of how much trust and commitment you score in the eyes of your customer. Trust and commitment equates to real engagement and that has some value points.

At key moments in the customer journey (especially where the customer makes a decision, acts upon a call to action, or enters into a transaction) the value points accumulate. Plot the value of each of those key moments in terms of how much it contributes to the overall journey and multiply up by a weighting of your top priority customers or customer segments.

The result will be a customer journey that shows where the most important points are for each top priority customer and how you are actually performing in their eyes.

That is real marketing measurement and you will never worry about vanity metrics again.

7.2 The practice of online measurement

In order for the effectiveness of digital marketing to be accurately analysed it is essential that any marketing activity meets the following criteria:

1. The marketing needs to have clearly defined success criteria
2. The call(s) to action need to be clear and unambiguous
3. There need to be effective means to track the customer path through the marketing activity to the desired end result
4. The collection and analysis of this data has to be cost-effective and timely

Corporate websites

For the vast majority of on-line marketing the company website is the chosen destination for the customers and this is the most mature field of on-line marketing. Therefore the majority of developments in on-line analysis has been in this area.

But how do you evaluate the effectiveness of your website? How do you improve its design?

The answer lies in web analytics – a whole new industry that has developed to measure and analyse internet data, bringing a new set of tools and jargon. It has a professional body – the Digital Analytics Association (DAA), with conferences, an education programme and standards for measures.

The Official DAA Definition of Web Analytics is: "the measurement, collection, analysis and reporting of internet data for the purposes of understanding and optimizing web usage."

Common measures
i) Online advertising
Key measures include:

Click through rate (CTR) – the percentage of viewers of an advert/marketing opportunity that make the first 'click' through to the target media. Within Pay Per Click advertising this metric rapidly identifies the initial success of any advert and is used by both the advertiser and publisher to select the best adverts.

Bounce rate – the percentage of viewers who initially click on an advert then immediately 'bounce' back to the originating website (or any other website). A high bounce rate indicates a poorly targeted advert.

Conversion rate – the percentage of viewers who subsequently complete the transaction to whatever is defined as a success by the advertiser (this is usually though not always a sale of some sort).

Cost per click – usually used with paid website adverts (adwords, etc) but can equally be used to assess the results of other marketing activities provided clicks can be attributed accurately.

ii) Email
The key measures used to analyse email effectiveness are:

Open rate – the percentage of subscribers who open an email

Click rate – the percentage who click on a link within the email

Unsubscribe rate – how many users unsubscribe from a mailing list

Bounce rate – emails that are 'bounced' back undelivered by the recipients' mail servers. This is similar to the rate of undelivered and returned mail with a physical mail drop. However once a link within an email has been clicked, any further 'bounces' refer to the act of the user returning immediately from the website.

A full list of all the terminology used within email marketing can be found at: http://emailmarketingpro.org/email-marketing-terms/.

It should be noted that most email marketing relies on tagging links and images with additional codes (or script) that is activated when the email is opened (and so requests images or code) and when links are clicked. Many email clients will automatically refuse to download images with tracking codes and so the Open Rate and Click Rate for email marketing are often large underestimates.

iii) Social media

Social media monitoring can provide organisations with a valuable insight into the views and opinions of their customers and users. It can offer the following:

- a cost-effective marketing mechanism;
- rapid feedback on advertising campaigns;
- a quick easy way to provide customer support and assistance; and
- a means to track commentary on the organisation and to act upon it if necessary.

Each activity requires different skills and tools to provide suitable results.

Marketing and feedback monitoring requires regular scheduled reporting of responses (both comments and click throughs). Customer support requires more real-time information and a search facility to ensure timely responses.

Legal Compliance requires both a real-time search facility for the 'live' social media sites but also an aggregator and search report function for blogs and other web publishing.

For most organisations the monitoring of social media will take place as an adjunct to regular clippings services or brand awareness exercises.

For monitoring of advertising response the contribution of social media monitoring will normally be a relatively minor element of the overall reporting (alongside focus groups, etc.) and so the majority of reports will be created in existing packages with social media becoming a data element rather than the primary source.

In these circumstances it is essential for established reporting packages to integrate data generated by social media. In reality Excel, PowerPoint and Word are likely to be the tools used to generate management reports and so, at this early stage of development, exporting of .csv files and graphs are likely to be the limit of integration.

Software products
The majority of social media tracking products are web based or 'cloud' based applications with both a free and subscribed element. For each organisation it is likely that a combination of live activity and off-line reporting functions will be required. The following tools are the current front runners in the social media management space.

Hootsuite www.hootsuite.com
Hootsuite was initially developed as a tracking system for Twitter but has now integrated a much richer range of social media sites. Its core differentiator is the reporting facility which can generate a wide range of reports on both trending, tagging and click-through success across multiple platforms and automatically send these reports to a designated user.

This automation increases consistency and ensures regularity of reports – essential for trend analysis and marketing campaign monitoring.

Tweetdeck www.twitter.com

Tweetdeck was originally a stand-alone organisation developing a third party front-end to Twitter. It quickly added extra links to other social media websites (it is interesting to note both which sites Tweetdeck and Hootsuite have invested in developing links to and also the overall strategy of Twitter to act as a funnel for content to its competitor sites.) It tends to be used primarily for heavy duty social media users to publish content rather than as a general monitoring tool but it does include a variety of live search facilities to enable users to monitor keywords, hashtags and trends. For day-to-day use it tends to be popular but as a business tool Hootsuite tends to have better functionality.

CoTweet www.cotweet.com

CoTweet (particularly the Enterprise Option) provides a very feature rich live monitoring and management facility for organisations with multiple social media presences and wishing to manage multiple conversations and support issues. @BTCare is a major user of this product for its live support services.

Reporting functions are similar to Hootsuite but are more focused on the internal social media space whereas Hootsuite also enables tracking of marketing activity outside SM sites.

Bitly www.bitly.com

Bitly.com is primarily a URL shortening service which is of particular use on Twitter. However it can be easily used on facebook.com. The key benefit of this service is the sidebar tool that allows users to browse sites then quickly share found URLs across their social media platforms.

The use of Bitly then allows companies to monitor and track any links to pages.

Twitterfeed www.twitterfeed.com

Twitterfeed is primarily a marketing tool as it allows bloggers to automatically share their blogs and/or websites through Social Media sites.

It uses RSS feeds to collate information and spread this through the social media space.

The key advantage for businesses is the ability to control, through a single gateway, how data is disseminated and this makes monitoring and tracking more consistent.

Shoutlet www.shoutlet.com

Shoutlet promises to combine all the functions of the current plethora of management tools into a single interface where content can be distributed and tracking of the resulting behaviour can then be managed and reported on in a single interface.

The core features include:

- Pre-scheduling of content – schedule status updates, tweets, video distribution, and Facebook tabs in advance
- Post to multiple platforms – post to Facebook, Twitter, and RSS feeds simultaneously with one click
- Complete Facebook management – design, moderate, and publish content to Facebook
- Moderate Facebook, Twitter, and YouTube – monitor and moderate Facebook communities with workflow management, comment responding, email notifications, and keyword filters
- Control user access levels: assign author, editor, and publisher level to members of your team

The reporting features mirror most of those available in Hootsuite though with a number of limitations relating to automation and customisation of reports to suit the organisation.

The market for social media monitoring tools is young and there are no established key players (unlike Web Analytics where Google Analytics is the major player by far). Most tools have grown from publishing interfaces with reporting being added as extras over time.

Of greater importance is the development of clear 'rules of engagement' within the organisation so that individuals understand the risks and limitations of their social media engagement. These rules of engagement should cover all parts of the organisation and should determine both the nature of interaction and also any escalation paths within the company should they be required. Most risks occur when individuals go 'off-piste' and attempt to act outside their experience and expertise.

Logfiles and tagging
Logfiles
Behind every website there is a computer server and inside every server there are log files which are a record of all web page activity.

Advantages of logfile analysis – the data is on the company's own servers, which makes it readily available. In addition, the format of the data is standard, so it can be manipulated more flexibly than if it was provided through a vendor with their own format. The benefit of this comes in the long term because the analysis of historical data can be carried out with whatever software is available. Some page tagging solutions have been accused of leading to 'vendor lock-in' where it is difficult to switch from one provider to another without substantial work.

Disadvantages of logfile analysis – conversely logfile analysis is criticised for providing inaccurate traffic figures. One reason for higher traffic readings is that pages are visited by robots in addition to humans. Software is programmed to 'trawl' the worldwide web continuously, particularly to update search engine databases and there are other reasons for 'spider activity' which include experimentation, competitive intelligence gathering and so on. Logfile analysis software cannot always distinguish human from robot activity.

A web page may not display fully before the user moves on to another website, this is not a 'view' but it is still recorded by a logfile. Page tagging detects if the page is viewed properly.

Typical topline logfile analysis – (from http://awstats.sourceforge.net/ demo at http://www.nltechno.com/awstats/awstats.pl?config=destailleur.fr)

A list of Free Log Analysers can be found at: http://www.prospector.cz/Freeware/Web-development/Log-analyzers/

Page tagging

A second method called Page Tagging (or JavaScript Tags) emerged as a new standard for collecting data from websites. A few lines of code are added to each page. When a page loads, these tags cause data to be sent to a data collection server.

There are three major search engines with advertising linked and thereby creating networks. These are Google, Microsoft (with Bing) and Yahoo.

Because tagging is visible to the whole world we can go to any website, inspect the code and discover which service is being used. The Vendor Discovery Tool by Web Analytics Demystified was written to automate the process. You can simply enter a web address into the software (perhaps one of your competitors) and the 'analytics vendor' is identified. This is a free and transparent service so we can see the last 100 site enquiries made. This is useful to see the importance of the different services. From this we also know that at least 10 out of 100 companies use two or more analytic services, this is a minimum figure because log file analysis use is not detected by the Discovery Tool. It is clear that 'free' Google Analytics dominates, but that the paid-for Omniture has a strong hold on the market place.

100 queries at the Vendor Discovery Tool in October 2010 (http://www.webanalyticsdemystified.com/vendor_discovery_tool.asp)

Digital dashboards

A digital dashboard is a central place where a marketer can see at a glance a range of information that helps them turn data into intelligence to inform their decision making.

Good decisions help to grow a business, reduce risk in an organisation and ultimately provide a better customer journey and marketing service.

If you are not watching then you cannot measure, and if you do not measure you cannot prove the return on your investment of time, resource and budget. If you can't do that then competitors will quite rightly steal business, customers and social media engagement.

What do you put onto your dashboard of things to watch, measure and analyse? Simply, put the things that matter – a balance of financial, marketing, innovative and process data that can feed upward to deliver your marketing goals and beyond to your organisational goals.

It is very easy to collect data. The skill behind effective dashboards is to measure things that help you to learn and improve and turn that data into decision making tools. To do this it is important to blend and integrate not only the hard numbers but softer, subjective measures that can often give a broader context as to why the numbers are as they are.

The very best digital dashboards also automate the data collection and reporting process, providing up to the minute, and sometimes real-time, feeds of information to both speed up tactical decision making but also fuel longer term strategic thinking.

Trends are important too. To see a piece of data in isolation and reporting a situation at a fixed point in time is unlikely to give a clear indication of the scenario. A dashboard that reports over set periods, again tied into the decision-making schedule, is far more likely to demonstrate fluctuations and trends from which improvements can be made.

The starting point in digital dashboard planning is to understand your overarching objectives. Strategic and tactical goals will help to identify the kinds of data and information that need to feed into the dashboard. This filtering process in itself helps you to ensure you are only including information that will actually help you.

With the proliferation of available data from the likes of the popular Google Analytics, you can literally become swamped by information. In good digital dashboard creation the 'less is more' principle really does apply.

Here are some examples of online Digital Dashboard services that should help you to understand both what is available today and importantly how they are evolving to provide marketers with powerful content feeds in the future.

MarketMeSuite
Positioned as a social media dashboard for small businesses MarketMeSuite helps to link campaign activity within Facebook and Twitter with email reporting and outcomes. It focuses heavily on the output of information rather than the reporting and integration with other activity.
Pros: Twitter and Facebook publishing, ease of use, joined up interface.

Cons: Lack of strategic focus, one-size fits all.

Google Analytics
World leading website analytics service providing broad ranging insights into website performance and customer journey tracking. Customised reporting and ease of integration into existing websites makes Google highly accessible for all sizes and types of organisation.
Pros: Ease of integration into existing websites, automated reporting.

Cons: Focus only on website objective data.

iDashboards

Visually inspiring dashboards for a range of industries and functions including marketing and sales. iPhone and iPad integration for real time reports on internal data. Drill down capability on each and every data set with full export facility.

Pros: Interactive and responsive interface, link to traditional sales and marketing methods, tactical and strategic integration.

Cons: Potential cost of website and social media integration.

LoopFuse

Marketing automation through a step by step process, from tracking website visits to conversion. Integration with salesforce.com and LinkedIn with varied levels of reporting.

Pros: Link with existing CRM, integrated email publishing, website analytics.

Cons: Set-up, visual reports.

PureShare

Enterprise level dashboards and analysis reporting from a business-wide perspective with website to CRM inputs from multiple sources.

Pros: Range of data feeds.

Cons: Set-up, complicated preparation, integration with social media.

MetricPulse

Simple and intuitive interface for reporting website and social media activity. Data focused rather than intelligent but allows for some monitoring of competitors in a real time interface.

Pros: Simple web-based interface, Google Analytics, Facebook, Twitter integration.

Cons: Lack of strategic focus, cost.

In the future we expect to see these and many other dashboard services fully embrace a link between digital and traditional marketing and sales activity to measure every step along the entire customer journey. When that happens we will truly be in a position to prove our return on investment.

Technicalities of dashboards

Dashboards are single computer screens containing visual displays of performance information, usually from several sources. They are important in Web Analytics because most services deliver information in the form of a dashboard, and this can be customised to meet your needs.

The dashboard is personalised for one person but several versions can be created from the same data-set because several users may have different needs. The Web Analytics dashboard is generally in real-time, with a delay of seconds; non-real-time displays may have a delay of 24 hours or 48 hours depending on the information sources and service used.

The term 'dashboard' was taken from the console found in every motor car. Here the marketing manager is in the 'driving seat' and should be able to see his situation at a glance. The marketing manager is expected to choose Key Performance Indicators (KPIs) that help understand whether objectives are being met.

Illustrated here is the standard Google Analytics dashboard which will be familiar to users of this service. Note that a line graph indicates fluctuations in traffic over the last month, important numbers show the number of visits, the number of page views, the number of pages viewed per visit. There is a world map indicating that most visitors come from the USA. We can scroll down and see more information. There are numerous opportunities to personalise the displays offered.

Dashboard design considerations

There are several steps necessary for effective dashboard design:

- Selecting correct metrics
- Selecting correct visual displays
- Arranging the metrics in a meaningful way

- Ensuring that important details are emphasised
- Installing 'alerts' to indicate changes that may require attention

Setting up your web pages for analytics

It is easier to set web pages up for analysis using Java Tracking Code rather than Log File analysis. Log File analysis requires a greater technical expertise, but the page tagging service manages the process of assigning cookies to visitors. Google Analytics is the most popular method and a typical set-up process is as follows:

1. Visit GOOGLE ANALYTICS at www.google.com/analytics
2. Click SIGN UP NOW (you will need a Gmail account)
3. Follow the instructions and seek any TUTORIAL HELP during your journey

Bounce metrics

For many years we have heard the term 'stickiness' used in relation to websites. If a website is sticky then we attract a visitor and keep them looking at our site; hopefully they will take some action such as requesting further information or placing an order. Web Analytics has a word to describe the opposite of stickiness – it is the word 'bounce'. Bounce, as we saw in Chapter 2, occurs when a visitor arrives at a web page then leaves the site, effectively a single visit.

A bounce rate of 67% means that 67% of visitors took one look at the page and decided it was not for them. Only a third of visitors decided to look further into the site.

This can be interpreted in many ways.

One interpretation is that "I have been promoting my website to the wrong people, I may have paid for the wrong 'keywords' or I may have given misleading descriptions in my pages or in the hidden messages I write for search engines". Another interpretation is "that my 'entry pages' are badly designed; I need to modify them to create something far more interesting".

Avinash Kaushik, an authority on bounce rates, said "It is really hard to get a bounce rate under 20%, anything over 35% is cause for concern, 50% is worrying" (Kaushik, 2007). However, specific pages, such as blogs and case studies, especially when used as a landing page within a customer retention campaign, see high bounce rates because the visitor is already very familiar with the content on other pages on the site or is just dipping in for breaking news. Bounce rates for information websites are notoriously higher than ecommerce pages as visitors dip in to gather breaking news and leave – the same goes for blogs which have high bounce rates.

It is therefore important to note that whilst bounce rate is a key performance indicator in website analytics it should be used in conjunction with other measures to give a well-rounded view.

Segmentation filters
As marketers we are all taught about "Segmentation, Targeting and Positioning". We must divide the population into groups, only then can we decide what targets to select. Once we have a target or several targets, we can then position our product in the mind of the prospect. Web Analysts have adopted the concept of 'segmentation'.

Segmentation bases available through web analytics

Segmentation type	Segmentation bases	Additional segmentation bases (which can be added using a form or adding a service)
Demographic	Language preference	Age Sex Education Occupation Social class
Geographic	Country Geographic region City Timezone	Postcode area Zip code area
Behavioural	Online purchases Page visits Bounces Conversion behaviour Previous website Referring website Browsing behaviour Keywords used Pages chosen Search engine used Hour of the day Mobile phone user Connection speed Browser used	Benefit sought e.g. loyalty
Psychographic		Lifestyle Personality
Geo-demographic		ACORN MOSAIC PRIZM

Table 7.1 Segmentation bases available through web analytics

Dashboards have a set of pre-defined segments and the opportunity to build more. Where segments are **not** available they can be created by presenting website visitors with a form and asking them to select an option such as job title or hobby.

Other non-standard segments can be created by purchasing and fusing data, as is the case with geo-demographic systems and some vendors have proprietary systems that extend segments.

Adding segments to the dashboard is as easy as dragging or clicking as we see below.

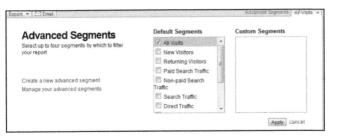

Figure 7.1 How to create extra segments (Google Analytics)

The figures below show how segmentation by mobile phone use and then geography appear on the visual display.

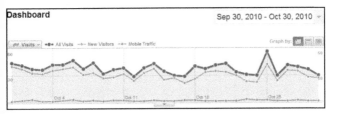

Figure 7.2 Dashboard showing mobile phone user segments

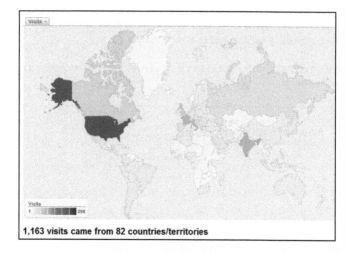

1,163 visits came from 82 countries/territories

Figure 7.3 Segmentation of visitors by country

It is interesting to see below that USA visitors have an average bounce rate (68%) but visitors from India are down at 50%. Here we see the value of applying the segmentation filter – it shows that Indians are more interested in the pages than Americans.

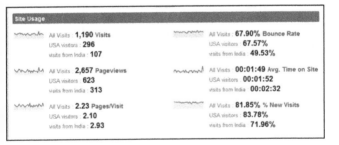

Figure 7.4 Segmentation of visitors by country

Site Usage

	All Visits	USA visitors	visits from India
Visits	1,190 Visits	296	107
Bounce Rate	67.90% Bounce Rate	67.57%	49.53%
Pageviews	2,657 Pageviews	623	313
Avg. Time on Site	00:01:49 Avg. Time on Site	00:01:52	00:02:32
Pages/Visit	2.23 Pages/Visit	2.10	2.93
% New Visits	81.85% % New Visits	83.78%	71.96%

Figure 7.5 Dashboard showing USA/India visitor bounce rate differences

Conversion metrics and testing campaigns

All websites have a purpose, and usually it is to persuade the visitor to carry out some action.

It might be:

- To read an article
- To sign up to a newsletter
- To request a brochure
- To make contact
- To place an order

When this objective is achieved, we can call it a conversion. Yes, the term 'sales conversion' springs to mind, but the web analytics use of the term can be stretched to other actions. One display option on most dashboards is the funnel.

Figure 7.6 shows a sales funnel used by the vendor Unica. If we follow it from the top we see that 2069 people entered an offer code, 473 started their shopping cart. There were some who abandoned their cart because 470 began the checkout but only 399 completed an order form.

We can substitute different actions at each point and instantly see the dropout at different points and 'fix' the problem. In this case there was something after the offer code that caused over 75% of people to go away.

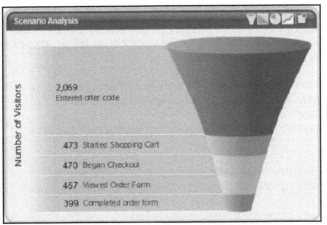

Figure 7.6 A sales funnel used by the vendor Unica

Funnels are often used in A/B Testing. Let's say we are testing two campaign approaches – one of the campaigns is centred on low price but the other on quality. We need to create two executions of a web page, one for each campaign, and the web server is told to alternate the viewing: so A goes to the first visitor, B to the second, A to the third and so on. Then a conversion funnel is created for both options and we can see the difference. This is simple but effective experimentation. Another test you may come across is MVA which means Multi-Variate Analysis, it goes beyond testing two versions (bi-variate analysis) and tests many aspects. Clearly this is a specialised field.

By setting clear objectives right the way through the conversion funnel journey the digital marketer is able to test and improve outcomes continuously in a controlled manner and thereby improve return on investment to the organisation.

Chapter 8: Legislation

Digital marketers must ensure they are familiar with and compliant with relevant legislation. In particular, you should become familiar with the key provisions of each of the following:

1. CAP Code, enforced by the Advertising Standards Authority (ASA) Since 1 March 2011, the non-broadcast Committee of Advertising Practice (CAP) Code has been extended to include marketing messages on businesses own websites, and other online content under their control.

This means that both paid-for and non-paid-for advertising and marketing online must now comply with the CAP Code. This includes:

- banner and commercial classified adverts - including adverts within emails
- pop-up adverts
- paid-for search listings
- paid-for listings on price comparison sites
- statements on your website intended to sell or promote your product or service
- sales and marketing messages on social networking pages under your control - e.g. Facebook or Twitter
- paid-for and non-paid-for sales promotions

However, the extended scope of the CAP Code does not include user-generated content on your website, or similar feedback on social networking sites - unless you incorporate it into your own marketing material.

2. The Distance Selling Regulations (DSR) and Electronic Commerce (EC Directive) Regulations 2002 (ECR) may apply if you are selling goods without a face-to-face interaction on the internet, by email or text messaging.

3. If you are not selling physical goods but are selling services, then the **Provision of Services Regulations 2009** apply instead.

4. If you are not trading to consumers but are purely business to business, then you need to check the **Business Protection from Misleading Marketing Regulations 2008** - but this is only really a problem if you are doing a lot of comparison of your products against competitors.

5. The **Privacy and Electronic Communications Regulations (PECR)** is the so called 'Cookie Law' but it also covers all electronic marketing communications including email, text, picture and video marketing messages, and WAP message. If you know the name of the person you are sending your electronic communication too, then the **Data Protection Act** also applies!

Further information on all of these can be found in the Law Handbook.

You should also be aware of the following:

Permission-based digital marketing
Organisations must research the needs and desires of their target audience and if appropriate various segments. Communications should be personalised and relevant wherever possible and have something new to say each time. Importantly from October 2003 an EU directive stated that prior to sending unsolicited email or SMS a specific and explicit 'opt-in' must have been received from the proposed recipient. In the USA an opt out law is proposed and this may legitimise spam (which currently makes up an estimated 80% of all email traffic).

Persistently offending organisations that do not comply with this legislation can be referred to ICSTIS and individuals may register with the telephone preference service (TPS) to cover opt-out of all such contact.

For more information: visit http://www.dma.org.uk

User generated content

From a legal perspective, User Generated Content (UGC) can cover Blogs, Forums, Video, Photographs, Audio, Software Code and other postings. UGC can encompass any content which users upload or post online. With such a wide array of UGC, there's an equally wide number of ways in which content on a website you own might contravene the law:

Copyright infringement is one of the most frequently mentioned legal issues in relation to sites like YouTube. Broadly, copyright infringement involves the unlicensed use of others' material and protected performance rights.

Defamation is another potential headache for site owners. In broad terms, this involves, 'the publication of a statement which tends to lower the claimant in the estimation of reasonable people'.

Moderation is an especially thorny issue affecting hosts of user generated content. In Europe the law is governed by the European E-Commerce Directive and implemented in the UK by the Electronic Commerce (EC Directive) Regulations 2002. This provides so-called 'safe-harbour' provisions for the providers of internet sites and services. Similar provisions exist in the US through the Digital Millennium Copyright Act.

While the legislation does not impose a duty upon website owners to monitor the activity of users, the Napster trial in the United States held that site owners have a duty to police their sites to the fullest extent possible. Website operators must also avoid any activities which could be deemed to encourage or authorise illegal activity. It is for this reason that Youtube in the UK has been pressured by the government and relevant lobby groups to be proactive in filtering illegal or harmful content over the internet rather than responding after the event.

Many Web 2.0 sites, such as Digg and YouTube, enable the users themselves to moderate the content of the site, reporting inappropriate or illegal content to the site owners. Other sites, such as CurrentTV, moderate incoming content before it is posted on the site.

Creative Commons (CC) is a non-profit organisation devoted to sharing creative works for people to legally use and share. The organisation is able to release certain copyright licenses known as Creative Commons licenses. These allow creators to stipulate and communicate which rights they reserve, and which rights they waive for the benefit of other creators.

Glossary

The following provides a glossary of some the key concepts in this Handbook:

Affiliate

An affiliate program is a revenue sharing program where an affiliate website receives a portion of income for delivering sales, leads, or traffic to a merchant website. Originally the merchant/advertising company 'paid per click' (see PPC below) so that every click from the affiliate website was paid for. Increasingly, the merchant 'pays per action' so that the affiliate website receives a fee for any sales.

Analytics

Web analytics is the measurement, collection, analysis and reporting of data to understand and optimise web usage. Web analytics can include data on the number of visitors, page views and click through on pages. See Chapter 7 of this Handbook for more details.

Behavioural Targeting

This is a controversial technique. Behavioural targeting uses information collected on an individual's web-browsing behaviour, such as the pages they have visited or the searches they have made, to select which advertisements to display to that individual. Advocates claim this is a legitimate form of targeting messages which prevents a user being bombarded with unnecessary advertisements. Critics argue it is an invasion of privacy. Least controversial is the use of Cookies (pieces of information generated by a Web server and stored in the user's computer, ready for future access).

The most controversial behavioural targeting company is Phorm an internet advertising technology company. Phorm's technology monitors internet users web surfing behaviour at the ISP level – a technique known as 'deep packet inspection', which has raised accusations of spying with some privacy activists.

Clickstream
The path a user takes as they use a website. This can be analysed to provide information on how effective the navigation and content of the site are.

Content Management
Content management supports the collection, managing, and publishing of information. A key element is version control, so that changing content is clearly controlled.

Convergence
This has two meanings:
1. Different media platforms carrying similar programming, for example a BBC programme watched on digital TV via broadcast or cable, and on an iPhone using iPlayer. Consumers as a result have much more flexibility in when and how they consume broadcast content.

2. Consumer devices becoming multi-functional e.g. still and movie cameras, telephones, GPS navigators, personal organisers and so on.

Display advertising
Traditionally, a form of advertising that contains text plus logos, photographs or other images, location maps, and similar items. Display advertising appears on web pages in many forms, particularly web banners (embedding an advertisement into a web page).

E-commerce
Buying and selling using digital and online methods.

E-mail marketing
Promoting products and services by email. Organisations should not send unsolicited marketing messages by email unless they have prior consent, recipients' details cannot be revealed on any emails, and there must be a valid address for people to opt out of receiving emails. Advantages are the instant delivery, the ease of tracking responses and the relatively low cost.

Advergaming
In-game advertising is placed in either casual games, gaming consoles or PC-based games.

Hosting
Companies offer web hosting when they put another organisation's website online. Companies that offer this service include http://www.123-reg.co.uk/web-hosting/.

Mobile marketing
Mobile Marketing is a set of practices that enables organisations to communicate and engage with their audience in an interactive and relevant manner through any mobile device or network (MMA, 2013)

Optimisation
This is the art of creating websites to perform the best for the user, providing information and, where appropriate, sales. SEO or Search Engine Optimisation aims to make a website appear higher in the search rankings.

PPC
Pay per click. Advertising on a website, typically a search engine, that presents a link to the advertiser's site if it matches keyword terms. Advertisers typically bid on keyword phrases and receive higher ranking placement the more they bid.

Responsive web design
Also called 'adaptive design', this approach delivers different content to web users according to the hardware they use for viewing e.g. PC, phone, tablet.

Social media
Social media are any online media that allow peer-to-peer communication and interaction. Examples include wikis, blogs, videosharing, photo-sharing, social bookmarking, online gaming such as World of Warcraft. Branded examples would be Facebook, Twitter and YouTube. Social media is also called User Generated Content.

Usability

Usability measures the quality of a user's experience when interacting with a product or system – whether a website, a software application, mobile technology, or any user-operated device. A good source of ideas on improving a website's usability can be found at: http://www.usability.gov/.

User Generated Content

User Generated Content appears on websites such as Amazon where the website is owned by Amazon but users are encouraged to post lists, recommendations and reviews. The website owner will usually moderate the content, either before it appears on the website (premoderated) or after it has been posted (post-moderated). Reactive moderation is where other users alert the website owner of an inappropriate post. For example of a company using this effectively, see the Dove campaign in the Companion.

Viral marketing

Viral marketing is also called 'word of mouth' marketing. It is a campaign that encourages people to talk about your organisation, product or service. Online, viral campaigns often use social networking sites (such as Facebook). For good examples of viral campaigns, see http://www.blogstorm.co.uk/the-top-10-viral-marketing-campaigns-ofall-time/.

References

Alexa (2013) Top sites, [online] http://www.alexa.com/topsites (Accessed 16 Sept 2013)

Associated press (2013) *Number of active users at Facebook over the years*, [online], http://news.yahoo.com/number-active-users-facebook-over-230449748.html (Accessed 16 Sept 2013)

Cavazza, F (2013) Social Media Landscape 2013, [online], http://www.fredcavazza.net/2013/04/17/social-media-landscape-2013/ (Accessed 16 Sept 2013)

Centre for Retail Research, (2013) *Online Retailing: Britain and Europe 2012* [online], http://www.retailresearch.org/onlineretailing.php (Accessed 16 Sept 2013)

Chui, M, Manyika, J, Bughin, J, Dobbs, R, Roxburgh, C, Sarrazin, H, Sands, G, Westergren, M (2012) *The social economy: Unlocking value and productivity through social technologies*, [online], http://www.mckinsey.com/insights/high_tech_telecoms_internet/the_social_economy (Accessed 16 Sept 2103)

Dixon, R (2011), The real digital divide, *Marketing Magazine*, January

ebiz MBA (2013) *Top 15 Most Popular Social Bookmarking Websites* [online] http://www.ebizmba.com/articles/social-bookmarking-websites (accessed 4 September 2013)

Graziano, D (2013) *Google+ seemingly still a ghost town; brands continue to prefer Facebook, Twitter*, BGR [online] http://bgr.com/2013/05/14/google-plus-analysis-users-brands/ (Accessed 4 September 2013)

Grunig, J.E. and Hunt, T.T. (1984), *Managing Public Relations*, Holt, Rinehart & Winston

Holt, R (2013) *Twitter in numbers*, [online]
http://www.telegraph.co.uk/technology/twitter/9945505/Twitter-in-numbers.html (Accessed 10 Sept 2013)

IAB (2013) 2012 *Full year digital adspend results*, [online]
http://www.iabuk.net/research/library/2012-full-year-digital-adspend-results
(Accessed 10 Sept 2013)

Kaushik, A (2007) Standard metrics revisited: #3: Bounce Rate, [online],
http://www.kaushik.net/avinash/standard-metrics-revisited-3-bounce-rate/
(Accessed 10 Sept 2013)

LinkedIn (2013) *About LinkedIn*, [online], http://press.linkedin.com/about
(Accessed 10 Sept 2013)

MMA, (2013) Mobile marketing, [online]
http://www.mmaglobal.com/wiki/mobile-marketing (accessed 16 Sept 2013)

Ofcom, (2013) *Over a third of people with a mobile use email on their
handset, while over a quarter download Apps or use IM* [online],
http://stakeholders.ofcom.org.uk/market-data-research/market-data/communications-market-reports/cmr13/telecoms-networks/UK-5.82
(Accessed 4 September 2013)

The Radicati Group Inc (2013) *Email Statistics Report, 2013-2017*,
[online] http://www.radicati.com/?p=9669 (Accessed 30 Sept 2013)

Richards, J J (2009) In-game Advertising, Facts are Stubborn Things,
[online]
http://community.advertising.microsoft.com/msa/en/global/b/blog/archive/2009/10/04/in-game-advertising-facts-are-stubborn-things.aspx
(Accessed 24 Sept 2013)

Shy, O (2001) *The Economics of Network Industries*, Cambridge
University Press

Smith P R (2011) *Marketing Communications* (4th edition), Kogan Page

SOSTAC® is a registered trade mark of PR Smith, author of The SOSTAC® Guide to Writing the Perfect Plan (eBook) available from www.prsmith.org and www.facebook.com/prsmithmarketing and Amazon.

Stelzner, M A (2012) *How marketers are using social media to grow their businesses*, [online] http://www.socialmediaexaminer.com/SocialMediaMarketingIndustryReport2012.pdf (Accessed 16 Sept 2013)

Technorati, (2011) *State of the Blogosphere*, [online], http://technorati.com/social-media/article/state-of-the-blogosphere-2011-introduction/ (Accessed 10 Sept 2013)

Tippexperience (2013) *Hunter shoots a bear*, [online], http://www.youtube.com/watch?v=4ba1BqJ4S2M (Accessed 4 September 2013)

TNS Digital Life (2011) [online], http://www.tnsdigitallife.com/

Watkins, T (2013) Suddenly, Google Plus Is Outpacing Twitter To Become The World's Second Largest Social Network, [online] http://www.businessinsider.com/google-plus-is-outpacing-twitter-2013-5 (Accessed 10 Sept 2013)

Additional Reading/Sources

Marketers should consider the following links to more detailed information references include:

The Digital Analytics Association (DAA)
http://www.digitalanalyticsassociation.org

A proposed code of ethics
http://waablog.webanalyticsassociation.com/2010/09/web-analytics-code-ofethics.html

Free visitor counters to add to your web pages
http://www.website-hit-counters.com/
http://www.free-counters.co.uk/
Web Analytics Demystified: free cases, whitepapers even books!
http://www.webanalyticsdemystified.com/content/index.asp

Vendor discovery tool
http://www.webanalyticsdemystified.com/vendor_discovery_tool.asp
Website health check up, free. Try it now
www.bartlettinteractive.com/evaluator

Google analytics website
http://www.google.com/analytics/
Yahoo Analytics Website
http://web.analytics.yahoo.com/

(Google) Insights for search
http://www.google.com/insights/search/#

Google Trends
http://www.google.com/trends

Microsoft Analytics links
https://adcenter.microsoft.com/
http://en.wikipedia.org/wiki/Microsoft_adCenter
http://advertising.microsoft.com/uk/learning-centre/search-advertising/
adcenter-whats-new

Cosenza, V (2013) *World map of social networks*, http://vincos.it/world-map-of-social-networks/

Books
Arikan, A. (2008) Multichannel Marketing, Metrics and Methods for On and Offline Success, Sybex

Bradley, N. (2010) Marketing Research, Tools and Techniques, Oxford University Press

Clifton, B. (2008) Advanced Web Metrics with Google Analytics, Sybex, Wiley

Kaushik, A. (2007) Web Analytics: An Hour a Day Sybex, Wiley

Kaushik, A. (2010) Web Analytics 2.0 Sybex, Wiley

Mortensen, D. R. (2009) Yahoo! Web Analytics, Sybex, Wiley,

Peterson E.T. (2004) Web Analytics Demystified: A Marketer's Guide to Understanding How Your Website Affects Your Business, Celilo Group Media

Peterson E.T. (2005) Website Measurement Hacks, O Reilly e-book

Sterne, J. (2010) Social Media Metrics, How to measure and optimise your marketing investment, Wiley, New Jersey

Index

Cambridge Marketing Handbooks

This Digital Handbook is one in a series of Handbooks for marketing practitioners and students, designed to cover the full spectrum of the Marketing Mix. The other Handbooks include:

- Products
- Pricing Points
- Communications
- Services
- Philosophy
- Research
- Distribution
- Law
- Stakeholder